# EMPIRES OF DIRT

And you could have it all,
My empire of dirt…

*Nine Inch Nails*
*Johnny Cash*

"My name is Ozymandias, king of kings;
Look on my Works, ye Mighty, and despair!"
Nothing beside remains. Round the decay
Of that colossal Wreck, boundless and bare
The lone and level sands stretch far away.

*Percy Bysshe Shelley*

Behold, the nations are as a drop of a bucket,
And are counted as the small dust of the balance:
Behold, he taketh up the isles as a very little thing.

*The prophet Isaiah*

*Acknowledgements:*
Many thanks are due to Steven Wedgeworth, whose careful editorial work is most appreciated. ~ D.W.

Published by Canon Press
P.O. Box 8729, Moscow, Idaho 83843
800.488.2034 | www.canonpress.com

Douglas Wilson, *Empires of Dirt: Secularism, Radical Islam, and the Mere Christendom Alternative.* Copyright ©2016 by Douglas Wilson. Edited by Steven Wedgeworth.

Cover design by James Engerbretson. Front cover painting: "The Wreck" by Knud-Andreassen Baade (1835).
Interior design & illustration (Chester Cathedral window) by Valerie Anne Bost
Unless otherwise noted, all Bible quotations are from the King James Version.

Printed in the United States of America.

*Library of Congress Cataloging-in-Publication Data:*
Wilson, Douglas, 1953- author.
Empires of dirt : secularism, radical Islam, and
    the mere Christendom alternative / Douglas Wilson.
Moscow : Canon Press, 2016.
LCCN 2016027445 | ISBN 9781591281436 (pbk.)
LCSH: Christianity and politics. | Exceptionalism—United States. |
    Religious fanaticism—Islam. | Apologetics.
Classification: LCC BR115.P7 W497 2016 | DDC 261.7—dc23
LC record available at https://lccn.loc.gov/2016027445

16 17 18 19 20 21 22 23        10 9 8 7 6 5 4 3 2 1

# EMPIRES OF DIRT

*Secularism, Radical Islam, and
the Mere Christendom Alternative*

Douglas Wilson

*Edited by Steven Wedgeworth*

canonpress
Moscow, Idaho

*This book is for my grandsons—*
*Knox, Judah, Rory, Seamus, Titus, Shadrach, and Moses.*
*I trust that you will be faithful in the fight*
*long after I am gone.*

# CONTENTS

# INTRODUCTION: CATHEDRALS OF THE NEW FOUNDATION

I n the past, it is true, I have occasionally written positive things about generally despised groups. I have done this with the medievals, with the Puritans, and even for some aspects of the Confederacy. Given this propensity of mine, was it not just a matter of time before I would come out to praise some aspect of the dissolution of the monasteries?

The word *praise* overstates it, but should we not be more suspicious than we are whenever we find a general consensus of unexamined condemnations? In England, the cathedrals of the Old Foundation were the ancient structures that were built before Henry VIII took money from said monasteries and . . . built the cathedrals of the New Foundation. Those new cathedrals were at Chester, Gloucester, Peterborough, Bristol, and Oxford. The point to be made here is not that the dissolution of the monasteries was praiseworthy through and through. Nor is it that certain individuals did not feather their own nests significantly, which they certainly did. My point is a simple one—contrary to popular perceptions, the money from the dissolution was not *entirely* spent by corrupt barons binge drinking in their ancient manorial halls. Some of it—five cathedrals worth, at any rate—came from the Church and went to the Church. This may be faint praise, and that is all it is intended to be, because the only thing I am really after here is a metaphor for what we need to be doing now.

We need a Christendom of the New Foundation. I am speaking historically here, and not theologically. Theologically, Christ is the cornerstone (Acts 4:11), and there is no need for a new foundation—there can be no new foundation in that sense. The apostles and prophets are the foundation stones that God established together with Christ for the building of His Church throughout all ages (Eph. 2:20). In this sense, Christendom will always be a Christendom of the Old Foundation.

But historical circumstances change. There are times when we must regroup, take stock, and start over. Without abandoning any of the fundamental assumptions that all Christians should share, we must still recognize the differences between ages and labor from where we are, not from where we wish we could have been.

It is my contention that the centuries of secularism we have been dealing with, and more than this, the centuries of secularism that Christians have made an accommodation with, have gotten us *a peculiar form of bankrupt wealth*—kind of like the monasteries. What is needed is for us to figure out a way to take the inheritance that we have received from secularism, and to build churches with it. This Christendom of the New Foundation I am proposing will be a *mere Christendom*. But what do I mean by that?

In his engaging and admirable book *Bad Religion*, Ross Douthat mentions me in an aside,[1] and in that particular citation, he touches on a few things that need to be addressed at the very outset of any argument for a mere Christendom. They can be grouped under the heading of proposals that no one should be making and, if they are, they should stop it. But at the same time, the boys down in the secularist ministry of propaganda are dead set to make sure that any proposals that recognize that secularism is turning out to be pretty lame get accused of these things. In other words, Douthat is quite right that we shouldn't be doing the things we will invariably be accused of doing—provided we are doing something appropriate instead.

Certain things sound pretty scary, and theocracy is one of them. Douthat says that at times I have flirted with theocratic sentiments. It would be closer to the mark to say that—provided the necessary qualifications are made—I have been a

---

1 The quotes on this page and the next come from Ross Douthat, *Bad Religion: How We Became a Nation of Heretics* (New York: Free Press, 2012), 281 ff.

full-throated advocate of theocracy. Theocracy is not, however, to be confused with "theocracy" or any other form of government contained within scare quotes, to which I am unalterably opposed. As will be argued at length later, all societies are theocratic, and the only thing that distinguishes them is which God they serve. I want a theocratic society that maximizes human liberty, including liberty of consciences, and since this is a good thing, this means that we have to worship the God who gives all good things, the true and living God.

The second thing that concerns Douthat is the trap of separatism—a move which results in "paranoia, crankishness, and all the other pathologies of the religious ghetto." When the world gets too big and bad, the temptation for believing Christians is to withdraw to their ghettos, compounds, and monasteries. This can happen two ways. The first is the move of the principled separatists, such as the Anabaptists pursuing a parallel culture to the "decadent American imperium." Douthat mentions Hauerwas as an example of this, not to mention the more radical separatists among the Amish and Mennonites. But he also cautions the "neo-Calvinist homeschoolers" in this same regard, and it is a caution worth hearing. The original idea was "don't retreat, reload," but sometimes the temporary calm afforded by reloading can turn into a *de facto* retreat. Kuyperian efforts to regroup really need to take care to not turn into something else.

And last, Douthat mentions my doughty claim to be a "paleo-Confederate." This was actually in the context of rebuffing the accusation that I was a neo-Confederate, yearning for a do-over at Gettysburg. But I would actually want to identify with men like T.S. Eliot or Eugene Genovese on this topic, and not the last three Grand Kleagle Wizards. I am so far out of touch with that world that I am not even sure how to spell Kleagle. But any person who proposes we go in a completely different direction than secularism urges needs to be ready for this part of it—the slanders will come, and some of those charges will *appear* to stick. That is part of the cost of doing business. In our day, there is absolutely no way to argue for any form of Christendom whatever without having to answer for the Spanish Inquisition, the Salem Witch Trials, the slave trade, and numerous other icky things. But by "answer for," I do not mean that we should argue that such things were the bright sunbeams of history, lighting up our path along the way—although that will be what we are accused of doing. All you have to do is put any of those atrocities in some sort of context and you will be accused of being a strident defender of them. The atrocities of Christendom (which have been grievous when compared to the holy law of God) still pale in comparison to the great pyramid of skulls that the secularists have constructed. Understandably, they don't like having that pointed out, and have managed to make the *tu quoque* fallacy their ultimate defense.

But all this is necessary, I would argue, because secularism is on its last legs, and we will have to do something. But how is this possible to say? There are a number of ways this argument can be made, but allow me to point to just a couple. These indicators are not my own private claim to be able to

see the future, as though I had a crystal ball, but rather indicate which way I see certain important currents running.
The things I am pointing out do not seem to me to be dis-
putable, and it also seems obvious to me that they are highly
significant.

First, the anemic response of the secularists to the idea
of sharia law has been quite striking. For example, consider the various accommodations to forms of sharia law that
have been made around Europe. And through recent years,
when I have pointed *that* out, the laughter and the chortling
have been quite patronizing. "That couldn't happen here, you
boob." But then the encroachments of the advocates of sharia
law here proceed apace . . .

Now I know there is sharia law and there is sharia law.
There is the chopping off of hands and death by stoning, on
the one hand, and spiritual jihad against eating too much
cheesecake on the other. Given how human beings generally
spread themselves out across a range of opinions, it is not
surprising that some advocates of sharia law are not as out
there as others. But this distinction is one that secularism,
back in its robust and virulent phases, would have been incapable of making. This is the kind of reasonable distinction
that secularism can only make because it is in the process of
unraveling.

Think back to the days of the Christian reconstruction-
ists. Think of Ezekiel One-Tooth, living on his theonomic
compound somewhere in the Ozarks, unbending just a little,
in order to argue that the biblical requirement of death by

stoning could actually be met by a firing squad, for what are bullets, he asks, but very little stones? Meets the requirement, he says. And then put alongside him a moderate theonomist, a scholar and careful thinker like Greg Bahnsen, say. Do you think that as many secularists would be rushing to praise the "moderation" of Bahnsen the way they are defending the "moderate" advocates of sharia law? To ask the question is to answer it. No, what is happening is that self-confidence is draining clean out of secularism, as can be seen in their inability to take a clear, public stand against the encroachments of militant Islam. The pathetic European attempts to dab around the edges of this problem—by trying to ban burkas, for example—are a day late and a Euro short.

The second reason I would like to offer for considering secularism a spent force is that the devil is moving from opposing Christendom across the board to a more nuanced stance of supporting and advancing some forms of it. This will require greater development, but here is the outline of it.

When the Church crosses the border between "outside and persecuted" to "inside and influential," that border crossing does not mean that the devil has gone into retirement. He does whatever he can to prevent the formation of Christendom in the first place, but then, when it looks as though we are going to get ourselves some sort of Christendom regardless, he is concerned to manage what kind of Christendom we get. It was altogether a good thing that Constantine converted, and there was nothing bad about how the persecutions of the

Church ceased. Three cheers for all of it. But the spiritual war continued on, unabated.

Anybody who thinks that the apostle Paul would have had us put up a big "mission accomplished" sign on the aircraft carrier of truth at that point is seriously mistaken. Once we have Christendom, which the devil opposed, are there forms of it that provide him with a great deal of scope to continue his work? You bet.

And I have seen, in recent years, arguments from Christian scholars that, if adopted in the context of a renewed Christendom, would present a really big problem. In fact, they would be a problem in just the same area where people have accused Constantine. The idea is that Constantine wanted something to prop up the existing order and not something that would transform the existing order. Leave aside for the moment whether the accusation against Constantine is true. It is a plausible accusation nonetheless.

"Let's get Jesus to help us to succeed in what we were already trying to do." In a similar way, those Christian thinkers who want the lordship of Jesus Christ acknowledged in public affairs coupled with a continuation of soft socialism (e.g., N.T. Wright, William T. Cavanaugh) want something that cannot be. And when they get the former, what they want with regard to the latter will be completely undone. For someone like Eusebius, someone like James Madison turns out to be something of a letdown. Oh well, I would say.

So, then, the issues are perennial, but the terms are not. Anyone working through the tangled weave of religion and politics may need some help with terms. Anyone whacking away at the thicket of culture and faith with the machete of curiosity could probably use a simple lexicon. It seems only fair at the beginning here to provide some basic definitions.

I will be arguing throughout for the political expression of a mere Christendom. By *mere Christendom* I mean a network of nations bound together by a formal, public, civic acknowledgement of the lordship of Jesus Christ and the fundamental truth of the Apostles' Creed. I do not mean establishment or tax support for any particular denomination of Christians, but it is possible (and necessary) to avoid such establishment without falling for the myth of religious neutrality. Religious neutrality is an impossibility. So mere Christendom stands in contrast to sectarian Christendom on the one hand and complete secularism on the other. Approaching these alternatives from the middle distance are the claims of radical Islam, about which more in a minute.

*Secularism* refers to the idea, popular for the last few centuries, that it is in fact possible for nations to be religiously neutral. This impressive trick is managed by having everyone pretend that secularism does not bring with it its very own set of ultimate commitments. But it does bring them, and so secularism has presented us with its very own salvation narrative, in which story the Enlightened One arose to deliver us all from that sectarian strife and violence. The horse and rider were thrown into the sea, and this is why you can't put that Christmas tree up in the county courthouse.

American exceptionalism is the idea that America is a more of a creed than a nation. This kind of American exceptionalism makes a certain kind of civic religion possible, a quasi-sacramental approach which all consistent Christians reject as, in equal turns, blasphemous and silly. American exceptionalism in this sense is currently the high church form of secularism. American exceptionalism should not be defined as the grateful recognition that we live in a nation that has been enormously blessed in many ways. What might be called normal patriotism is not idolatrous, but is simply natural affection.

*Radical Islam* is a Christian heresy, but one of the features that it retained in its departure from the truth was the idea that religious claims are total and absolute. Islam functioned in this way for many centuries, competing head to head with the Christians, before the Enlightenment arrived in order to demote all forms of religious totalism (except for its own). Muslims who have accepted the claims of this secularism are now called "moderate" Muslims, while Muslims who are faithful to the older, all-encompassing claims of Islam are called radical Muslims. The word radical comes from the Latin *radix*, which means root. Radical Muslims have gone to the root of the matter, and they are the ones who at least understand the nature of the conflict. If Allah is God, then follow him. If he isn't, then we shouldn't.

And I would say the same thing about Jesus. If He is Lord, we should do what He says. If He is not, then we needn't bother.

# ANOTHER KIND OF
# AMERICAN IDOL

## AMERICAN IDOL

One of the greater threats to a healthy and normal patriotism is, not surprisingly, an unhealthy patriotism. There is such a thing as America-worship, and it is idolatry. Its existence and characteristics have been capably put forth in a recent book by David Gelernter called *Americanism*.[2] The first chapter of *Americanism* is entitled "I Believe in America," and it reveals the basic problem. A number of people have wanted to say that America is "dedicated to a proposition," and that we are not bound together by those common ties that bind other nations—mundane things like language, culture, music, food,

---

2  David Gelernter, *Americanism: The Fourth Great Western Religion* (New York: Doubleday, 2007).

and common descent. Because of this assumption, believing or not believing in America becomes a choice, like a religious choice, and that means you can fault people for not making it.

Wise people have always held back from blaming others for being born and raised in a different place. The providence of God has placed us in a certain position, and we should just deal with it. But religious claims, whether we are talking about the lordship of Christ, or whether Muhammad is Allah's prophet, or the noble eight-fold path of Buddhism–these are claims that can be adopted or rejected by anyone.

> 'I believe in America.' Many people have said so over the generations. They are not speaking of a nation. They are expressing belief in an idea, and not just any idea but a religious idea of enormous, transporting power.[3]

Gelernter takes this observation and makes a number of logical inferences from it. He says that "Americanism is a biblical religion,"[4] but note that this is *a* biblical religion, not *the* biblical religion. There are others—but it appears that they are all denominations within the broader scope of things, each with something to contribute. And it appears that compared to Christianity and Judaism, Americanism has the most of all to contribute.

Liberty, equality, and democracy (at least he didn't say *fraternity*) are the possession of all mankind, according to Americanism, and "Americans have a duty not merely to preach but to *bring* them to all mankind."[5] The Gettysburg Address is

3 Ibid., 1.
4 Ibid.
5 Ibid., 4.

"one of the most beautiful shrines mankind has ever seen, and one of the holiest."[6]

Here are some other gems:

> The American Religion is a biblical faith. In effect, it is an extension or expression of Judaism or Christianity. It is also separate from these faiths; you don't have to believe in the Bible or Judaism or Christianity to believe in America or the American Religion.[7]

> Most nations are based on no principles; they are based instead on shared descent or ethnicity. The United States is different.[8]

> You can believe in Americanism without believing in God—so long as you believe in man.[9]

This kind of thing takes the breath away, or ought to, and the initial reaction of many Christians will be to say that Gelernter must be a lone crazed neocon, and why are we paying attention to this? For several reasons, the first being that he is highly educated and competent. He is a professor of computer science at Yale, a contributing editor at *The Weekly Standard*, and a member of the National Council on the Arts. A number of the people mentioned in his acknowledgements are at the center of our national life, and not part of the Glazed Eye Set.

6  Ibid.
7  Ibid.
8  Ibid., 15.
9  Ibid., 20.

The second reason for taking him seriously *is that he is right*. Americanism has become a religion, and he accurately identifies how and where it happened. Where we should part company with him is to be found in his (religious) conviction that this development was a good thing. Faithful Christians will necessarily see it as a tragic fall into idolatry—and into one of the easiest forms of idolatry for conservative Christians to be tempted by.

He calls the Bible, rightly in my view, "the most important book in British and American history."[10] And tracing our emphasis back to the Puritans, Gelernter (again rightly) points to the refusal to exclude the Old Testament: "In *these* areas, Americans, reflecting Puritan practice, have often shown a surprising sympathy for the Old Testament view."[11]

Beginning in Britain, there was a strong tendency to identify the nation with a new Israel. This same tendency was transplanted across the Atlantic. Those familiar with how theology was done in the colonies are quite familiar with this marked feature. This is what lies behind William Bradford's phrase, "a city on a hill," which goes back to the gospel of Matthew and was picked up later by Ronald Reagan.

It was obvious to them that in the settlement of the New World, something big was in the works, and that they had a pivotal role to play.

"But America and Americanism are both impenetrable unless we start with the Bible. America's Puritans were

10  Ibid., 22.
11  Ibid., 24.

Christians who believed absolutely in the divinity of Jesus. But they were also obsessed with their role as the 'new chosen people' in the 'new promised land,' and they were fascinated with the Hebrew Bible."[12]

Gelernter also uses a phrase that Robert Frost used to describe his religious views to sum up this American sympathy, and I think it is quite accurate—"Old Testament Christianity."[13] This explains the development of what Gelernter calls "American Zionism." Chesterton once famously described America as a nation "with the soul of a church," and since the Church cannot be isolationist, neither can America be. Gelernter describes this as the impetus behind what he calls American chivalry. What goes on across the world is naturally our business. If we are St. George, then we shouldn't care where the dragon lives. So the question before the house then—are we really St. George?

What are we to say to all of this? Gelernter says that Americanism consists "of American Zionism and the Creed."[14] American Zionism is postmillennial wine turned to vinegar, and the Creed is a bastardized attempt to apply certain blessings found only in Christ to a civil order outside of Christ, a civil order which *rejects* Christ.

First, the Zionism. The Puritans thought of themselves as a new chosen people, settling into a new promised land. They held this in the context of a postmillennial vision of the gospel

12 Ibid., 32.
13 Ibid.
14 Ibid., 57.

extending to the ends of the earth. This Zionistic impulse is
why Americans tend to think that events on the other side of
the world are somehow our business and, if our business, then
shortly thereafter the business of the American military. The
Church believes this rightly, because Christ told us to take
the gospel to all nations. But secularize the doctrine and you
have Woodrow Wilson's foreign policy, which, incidentally,
has been the foreign policy of virtually *all* modern presidents.
If you want to know what postmillennialism looks like with
Jesus taken out of it, look no further than George W. Bush's
Second Inaugural.

The Creed, as Gelernter presents it, is "liberty, equality, democracy."[15] But if this is being presented to us as a series of
answers to basic religious questions, we need to be prepared
for the follow-up questions. Why should men be free? Why
should they be treated with equity? Why should we govern
ourselves democratically? The answers will vary depending on
whether you believe that we evolved out of the primordial
goo, or God put us here. They will vary according to whether
you believe in the Supreme Court or the Supreme Being. Religions don't do well suspended in midair. Why should men
be free? Who makes them free? How can they be free when
they are slaves to sin?

The problem is that any *biblical* response to all this should
be fasting and mourning. Gelernter's definition of a biblical
republic—a nation with the Bible on its mind—is extremely
problematic. I *do* think he is right that this is what we are.

15  Ibid., 69.

I believe we can extend Flannery O' Connor's observation about the South to the entire nation. We *are* Christ-haunted. But, as O' Connor clearly knows, and Gelernter does not acknowledge, this is hardly a good thing. Biblical phrases do reach us, and they do affect us. There remains a deep tradition of biblical influence, despite everything. But as the book of James teaches, the man who hears the word and does not do it *deceives himself* (Jas. 1:22).

This is where American religionists stumble. Try as we might, we cannot have the Bible without Jesus also. And we cannot have the Bible without running into all those places *where Jesus unambiguously condemns what we are trying to do*. Those who appreciate the Bible for its literary or historical value will not appreciate the Bible for long. And if they take the Bible on its own terms, then the syncretistic project proposed by Gelernter falls to the ground. This is why Americanism is an idol, and it is why those Americans "with the Bible on their mind" will be intensely interested in getting our ropes over its head and pulling this particular idol down.

Not only does the *Bible* condemn what we are doing, all those Puritans who set us on this course would also condemn what we are doing. Gelernter may appreciate *them*, but they most certainly would not appreciate him. They would rightly disown us. If we want a biblical pattern for this, let us go (as good Old Testament Christians) to the reign of Jeroboam who made Israel sin at Dan and Bethel (1 Kgs. 12:29).

Seeing ourselves as *a* new Israel (which is only OK if we refuse to claim that we are uniquely *the* new Israel) is a two-edged sword. We are not just a city on a hill; we are also (if we read the stories rightly) a city in ruins because of its gross idolatry. You cannot be a stainless steel Israel, incapable of apostasy. Israels don't come in that model.

Given the nature of this discussion, let me offer a disclaimer that I believe I will probably have to make over and over again. Lest I be accused of a lack of native affection, let it be noted that I love my country and am grateful to have had an opportunity to serve her in the Cold War. Not only so, but I am also *culturally* an American, and I like being that way. No complaints. No leftist America-hating here. Apple pie, red-checked tablecloth, and a Winchester over the fireplace. But to paraphrase Thomas Watson, we can receive gifts from Christ without making a Christ out of our gifts.

But Gelernter is not some lone idolater doing weird things—like the first Elvis worshiper or something. He has a great deal of company, and I believe that he is correct that a large number of people *do* subscribe to his Creed and are willing to export it as a spiritual duty. Gelernter quotes Woodrow Wilson to this point: "I believe that the glory of America is that she is *a great spiritual conception . . . .*"[16]

What Gelernter is trying to do is provide American Christians with an amalgam—keep your Christianity private, and Americanism will fill the public void. Christians do have an instinctive need to see public justice, but virtually all American theologies from all our Christian denominations *prohibit this*. Wall of separation, two kingdoms, rapture any minute,

16 Ibid., 156. Emphasis mine.

and many other foglike words. And so the naked public square is being filled with political idols, and American Christians are being told that these public idols are somehow consistent with our private worship of the true God. *But they are not.* And the only way out of this impasse is to acknowledge that Jesus Christ is Lord of these United States.

Gelernter says, "If there is to be justice in the world, America must create it."[17] When I read things like that, I usually have my *jumpin' Jehoshaphat* reaction. Did he really say that? Yes, he did, but the reason he is able to get away with it is because of the massive loss of confidence and faith that Christians have in Scripture. How can we be appalled when he says that if we are not willing to counter immediately with, "No, if there is to be justice in the world, and in this nation, Jesus must do it"?

## THE IDOLATROUS NARRATIVE

*Idolatry is an account of the world.* It is not stand-alone worship of some god who is not God, who is being worshiped for its own sake. No, the idol is connected to an account of the *world.* This means that when we reject the idolatry, as we must do, we are still not in a position to reject the thing of which that idol is erroneously thought to be lord. We reject Aphrodite, not sexuality. We reject Mammon, not the money in our wallets. We reject Ceres, not wheat farming. We reject Poseidon, not joining the Navy.

Bringing it home to our point, we reject John Stuart Mill, not liberty. We reject Ayn Rand, not liberty. Indeed, if we

17 Ibid., 205.

understand what the Spirit of God is doing in the world (2
Cor. 3:17), we reject idolatrous accounts of individual freedoms *because* we love liberty. I look dubiously at the shaman
who shuffles around in a heathenish circle shaking his rat-
tle, but I must still receive the rain with gladness. If I reject
the rain because of the shaman, then I am actually rejecting
Christ (Acts 14:17).

What would I think of someone who said that I shouldn't
be using that rain on my crops because of the pagan dance?
No, I reject the pagan *account* of the rain, and I reject the pagan *ceremonies* to summon the rain, but I must not reject the
rain. Rain is good.

In the same way, individual liberty is a good thing, a blessed
thing. It is a gift of God and can only be sustained over time
when a people extend gratitude to the one who gives it to us.
Secularism, in all its forms, is therefore the enemy of liberty. Some forms of secularism set themselves against liberty
overtly—the idols of the collective, for example. We oppose
them, too, because we are anti-Communists, and we are anti-Communists because we love Jesus. Other forms of secularism set up a goddess of liberty over against the collective,
and we reject that form of idolatry also. We reject the god
of chains, because he will put us in chains, and we reject the
goddess of untrammeled liberty and autonomous individual
freedoms . . . because she will put us in chains.

Christians are called by Christ to infiltrate every level of
every society they find themselves in, and to do so *without* the
idolatrous commitments that surround them on every hand.

If they are living in a time of empire, it is not ungodly com-promise with empire to do this—think of Daniel and Joseph, just for starters. At the same time, temptations to capitulate before the idolatrous pretensions will be common enough—think of Daniel's three friends.

It is possible to render *subordinated* honor that is not idol-atrous. Not only is it possible to do, it is necessary to do. But in order for this honor to be a biblical civil honoring, words like *sacred*, *hallowed*, and *religion* must be kept entirely and completely away from it. There must be a sharp line of de-marcation that separates the kind of honor that is due to a nation and its magistrates and the kind of honor that belongs to God alone. That line of demarcation must be maintained by the kinds of words we use and will not use.

For example, suppose that some members of the American military are guilty of war crimes. Leftists will say that these soldiers sinned against humanity, and that this is a character-istic sin that Americans tend to commit. The right-wingers will say that they sinned against America, and that this was uncharacteristic of our soldiers, and they will go on to say that the sin was one of being un-American.

But such things are sins, if they are sins at all, only if they are ungodly. And we can only know what ungodliness is if God communicates to man, and man is responsible to listen and to hear. The most basic question for those seeking to live an upright life has to do with how we go about defining upright. *By what standard?* As the debate escalates, the talking heads on television are going to become the yelling heads on television. Stop listening to what they are saying, and start asking what they are sitting on behind those television desks. What is their basis for being there? What supports them such that the camera can point at their faces?

When the leftists call this a crime against humanity, I will want to know what they think humanity actually is. The end product of so many millennia of mindless and purposeless evolution? It would seem to follow that these soldiers committed "crimes" against so many pounds of protoplasm, of which we have plenty on this planet. Indeed, liberals like to tell us all the time that we have way too much of this bipedal kind of protoplasm. War is just a drastic eco-measure, and these soldiers were just going green.

When the right-wingers tell us that this was un-American, we should want to know why *that* is a problem. Wiener schnitzel is un-American. Simply being un-American is not a moral issue. No, no, they might say. "We didn't say not American, we said un-American. There's a difference." Oh, I would reply. Tell us that difference, and tell us why we should care. Tell us how America has generated a moral code that is universally binding on all who are associated with this nation. Try not to suspend that universal moral code from an invisible sky hook or, worse, from snippets of the Gettysburg Address that you learned as a child in an American elementary school.

One of the things that Jesus taught us is that a house cannot withstand storms without a foundation (Mt. 7:24–25). You cannot build your house in a left wing swamp or on a pile of right wing sand and then, when troubles arise, as they surely will, whistle up the foundation you wish you might have had. You either have a foundation when you need it, or you don't.

This is why it is important that we have certain inalienable rights that our *Creator* gave us, and not rights that were bequeathed by the latest referendum, or by the kindness of the king. If the Lord gives, only the Lord can take away. If the State gives, then the State can take away, and blessed be the name of the State.

The point here is that the biblical Christian has a natural point of appeal above every human institution—whether that institution be popular elections, that fortress of fraud we call the Congress, the faux-imperial White House, or the black-robed SCOTUS Nazgul who ghoulishly prey on the unborn. One of them singly, or all of them together, can be withstood by one courageous man with an open Bible. "You may not, as Yahweh reigns, do this thing." To take such a stand would require courage, as John the Baptist had to have in order to rebuke Herod, but to take such a stand cannot depend on a convoluted set of political contradictions. Life is simple. God outranks the king. The king is to do what God says, not the other way around. "What a strange religion you Christians have!" I can hear someone saying.

But for the secularist, what outranks the highest human authority? What text can a secularist point to when he is trying to stand against certain democratic measures? It matters not if the democratic measure is a great idea or a howler. So long as he differs with it, it should not matter to him if the people are voting to close Home Depot on Sundays, or if they are not suffering a witch to live. There is no God above the people, right? Imagine there's no heaven; it's easy if you try.

So he considers those measures extreme. But define "extreme," and there's the rub.

## PROPHETIC AND BALANCED BOTH

Having said all this, we still have to keep our sense of balance. When Constantine was converted, there were Christians who exhibited more than a little Eusebian exuberance, saying glowing things that ought not to have been said about any mortal man. At the same time, they were saying them in a time when the really serious idolatry had been dealt its death blow. History reveals that they were a bit too giddy, but, by and large, it was Christians like that, giddiness and all, who had brought down pagan Rome.

The statists who support Obama and the statists who are disillusioned with him because he has not pressed for the complete package, the complete totalitarian hellhole, are serious idolaters. The household gods of the American right that get a pinch of salt every now and again are a real irritation, a real compromise in the Church, and every worthy preacher ought to direct sermonic haymakers at such compromises at every appropriate opportunity. *Stop* it.

At the same time, that worthy preacher must distinguish serious statism from this lump-in-your-throat nationalism. He must distinguish the superstition of the grandmother who leaves out saucers of milk for the kitchen fairies and the priest with bloody robes who demands your firstborn for Molech. Just as the true faith has its spice-rack tithing and its weightier matters, so also do those who worship idols.

So how does this figure in with a discussion of mere Christendom? One of the central characteristics of our cultural disease is our societal relativism. This is the end result of what C.S. Lewis called the poison of subjectivism, and it results in the abolition of man. "Woe unto them that call evil good, and good evil; that put darkness for light, and light for darkness; that put bitter for sweet, and sweet for bitter!" (Is. 5:20).

But this moral inversion is not something that can be achieved in a day. Before you reverse good and evil, you must flatten good and evil, and before you flatten good and evil, you must flatten greater evil and lesser evil and greater good and lesser good. Moral egalitarianism is a rot that proceeds slowly.

Woe unto them that call lesser evil greater evil, and greater evil lesser evil; that put darkness for twilight, and twilight for darkness; that put white for off-white, and off-white for white!

Now when God's representatives speak to the civil ruler, they are speaking prophetically. And when the prophets of God speak, they must represent Him well. If *He* does not lose a sense of proportion in the Day of Judgment, then His representatives must not "get to preaching" in such a way as to get carried away. And they must not get to denouncing sins in such a way as to create a moral equivalence between excessive consumerism on display at Radio Shack and Stalin's genocidal technique of artificial famine. They must not flatten the abortion holocaust and extra questioning at the airport for a guy named Muhammad.

Those who draw glib examples of moral equivalence between full-throated pagan societies and raggedy Christian ones are *people whose judgments are not to be trusted.* Someone once wisely said, about another issue, that if your pastor says that wine in the Bible is actually grape juice, then why should you trust *anything* he says?

The same principle is operative here. Jesus calls men "fools and blind" over just this principle. They did not know up from down. They did not know whether the gold sanctified the altar or whether the altar sanctified the gold. They could not tell a gnat from a camel. *They did not have a sense of proportion.* They tithed out of their spice rack and neglected the weightier matters of the law (Mt. 23:23).

This is why so much of the contemporary "prophetic" witness to our civil rulers is such a joke. It not so much dressed in camel hair with a leather belt as it is decked out in some Kuba the Clown outfit. And *then* it blames the lack of responsiveness on hardness of heart, and walks off saying *o tempora! o mores!* in a Donald Duck voice.

## CHRISTIANS AS DUTIFUL SONS

Christian patriots are the ones best suited to help America in her current idolatrous impasse. In my experience, those who are most ambivalent or cynical about patriotic pieties—flags, fireworks, and fun—are most likely to support the abuses of statist power when the state is attempting to become some jitney god in the lives of its citizens. But those who wave the flag at the parade and eat their hot dogs afterward are most likely to recognize that the government has gotten itself way out of line. Take a couple big E on the eye chart issues—homosexual marriage and abortion. Take a poll of a thousand people at a Fourth of July parade, where flags are everywhere, and then poll the same number of people who would not dream of attending such a cheesy event. Which group is most likely to support the oppressive tyranny, right or wrong, and which group is most likely, overwhelmingly, to oppose it? Right.

Say that Mom has a drinking problem, and it is time for an intervention. Whom do you want leading and coordinating it? The son who calls every week and sends flowers and a card every Mother's Day or the son who has been a cynical smart-mouth from high school on? The son who has observed the pieties is *qualified* to say something about the maternal sin and is the most likely to do it right. The other son might actually be the source of the problem and ought not to be put in charge of fixing it.

Pride is the wrong word to use, but I am extremely grateful to be an American. I really like it. As noted earlier, I cultivate my affection for apple pie, and I really do own a Winchester rifle. On the Fourth, I love to barbeque some burgers and dogs and then head off to set off some fireworks—not just as a fun display for the grandkids, but to commemorate an important historical event. I did my stint in the Navy, and I have seen the former Soviet Union through a periscope. I really like the sense of place and family that pervades country music. I enjoy mowing the lawn, football in the fall, and voting the bums out. I honor the flag.

For the cynic, all this "sentimentalism" amounts to compromises with the local Baals. I might worship Yahweh in Jerusalem, they would say, but here in our little valley, I doff my baseball cap when I walk through the local groves of the Ashtoreth.

Not a bit of it. My natural affection for my people and place—which every Christian must cultivate in *his* place, for *his* people—does not interfere with my ability to challenge the regnant follies, insanities, and cruelties. That natural affection, that patriotism, is actually one of my *qualifications* for doing so. We have plots currently afoot in Washington that George III would not have countenanced in his nightmares. And if I go to a big rally dedicated to telling the federal government to stop acting like a colony of Mordor, I am willing to bet you that, as I make my way through the parking area, I will spot an awful lot of the pick-up trucks with American flags on them.

There are many reasons for my behavior on this theme of mere Christendom, but one of them is that the concept provides the only real antidote to American exceptionalism on the one hand and radical Islam on the other. We are constantly and regularly subjected to a false alternative. Either we must believe that America is the last best hope for mankind, or we must be muttering ingrates who don't recognize or appreciate any of the advantages of living here. As Digory would say, "Bless me, what do they teach them in these schools?"

America is emphatically not the last best hope of mankind. What perfect nonsense. Jesus is the Savior. He is the last Savior, He is the best Savior; He is the blessed hope.

But America is emphatically not a dingy little tawdry place to live in, either. It is a great nation, and has accomplished many great things—as other great nations have done before us and as yet others will after us. Israel is set before *all* of them as an example. We are not loved because we were mighty. We are mighty because we were loved (Deut. 7:7). Muddling that order up is a very dangerous thing to do (Deut. 8:10–19), *and a lot of our so-called conservatives are doing it.*

At the same time, this is a wonderful place to live, still, but the rot has, in fact, set in, and there are already other places in the world where it would be better to live than certain parts of our nation. Some of our states are completely addled and deranged and have labored energetically to become banana republics. Recent elections show that New York and California richly deserve, good and hard, everything that's coming to them. What happened to Californian exceptionalism? Where did it go?

Now I am most grateful to God for the kindness He showed in placing me in this nation. But gratitude is not pride, and this is a nation of sinners, prone to do what sinners in this position have always done—which is to interpret blessings as rewards, to see the milk and honey as "best in show" indicators. The reason this is a big deal is that the very quickest way to shut off God's favor, like you were turning the spigot hard to the right, is to start to take credit for gifts.

Christians have long spoken of the temptation to focus on the gifts, forgetting the Giver. As a nation, we are a stage beyond that. We have forgotten the Giver and are bragging about the gifts. The fact that the leftists sneer at the gifts is their problem. They should confess their sins, just as we should confess ours.

But this is the cul-de-sac that secularism has created for us. If we cannot publicly honor the God of all nations, and Jesus the Prince over all nations, then everything has to be measured "under the sun." In the first place, under the sun everything is vanity and shepherding wind, as someone tried to teach us once. In the second place, the nation who holds first place in the present moment, for there is no other moment, has to act as though *that* is the ultimate vindication—which it is, until the next ultimate vindication of somebody else. And the next, and by the time we are three down the line, we have become one with Nineveh and Tyre. If we don't repent of this foolishness, then God will settle our hash.

## TAKING AMERICA BACK . . . TO THE GOSPEL

A common rallying cry for conservative activists, including Christians, is that we need "to take America back." OK, sign me up. Take America back *where*?

Generally the point is that we need to take America back *from* the liberals and progressives—the secularists in the academy, the homosexuals in the streets, and the raunchy movie producers in our very own Netflix queue. OK, sign me up again. Once we have taken America back *from* those guys, what do we do with it? The assumption is that the underlying America is just fine the way it is unless some progressive has been messing with it. We need to "save America," the thinking goes, and so the language of salvation is used all the time. But in our heart of hearts, we think we are saving an innocent kidnapping victim, and not a skid row bum who became a drunk because of his own stupid choices.

In other words, once the progressives, that *alien* force, are taken out of the picture, America's native good sense will return, the nation will right itself, common sense will again prevail when it comes to the national budget, we will stop killing the unborn "because we are too good for that," and so on. In short, America gets to be saved without a savior. America gets to be saved without repentance. America gets to be saved without hearing and believing the gospel. In other words, if the terms of the Great Commission were a great tournament, America always gets a bye.

This is not just a trivial error; it is heresy. It is another gospel. It is false and damnable. Further, it is a basic reason why we have so little success in fighting the progressives, whose vision for society really is a lunatic vision. Traditional values can't fight sin, for the same reason that healthy tissue can't fight cancer, but is rather the tissue that provides cancer with its scope and its future.

You can tell this assumption is operating when somebody says that progressive socialism is "un-American." No, our leftists are homegrown, and every bit as American as, say, an amber wave of grain. To return to the cancer illustration, what good does it do to say that this cancer is not "*my* cancer"? It shouldn't kill you then, right? To say this cancer in my body is not *my* cancer, but is rather some kind of "European-style" cancer makes no sense, other than perhaps as an exercise in blame shifting.

If you persist in saying that the healthy tissue is the "real you," and that the moral cancer rotting out your bones is not the "real you," then this precludes repentance. And yet, the declaration of the gospel—that Christians were told to preach to all nations, including *ours*—includes preaching repentance and faith. Nations means nations, repentance means repentance for our own sins and not other people's, and faith means faith in Jesus Christ. Baptism means baptism into the name of the Father, Son, and Holy Spirit. Sorry to get into all the deep theology here but the Christian faith means calling everyone to believe in Jesus. The name for not wanting to do that is *unbelief*.

This is what we must do in order to "take America back." Any attempt to take America back without an explicit call for America to become (again) a Christian nation is an exercise in futility, and far from taking America out of the saloon, it is actually buying her another drink.

I am not calling for America to join a particular denomination. This is by no means sectarian. I am simply saying that our nation—our leaders, our judges, our poets, our jesters, and our people as a whole—must confess that Jesus is Lord. They must confess that *only* Jesus is Lord. Other nations are called to do the same and, as they do, they would of course recognize one another as sister nations in Christ.

This is what I would call mere Christendom. These are the cathedrals of a new foundation. And this is what I want to argue for in this book.

# CHRIST AND CULTURE

few years ago I was reminded, yet again, of the central heresy of our age. The president, in his Easter address, called upon all of us to remember our "shared spirit of humanity," and he trotted out that tired "family of man" stuff. It doesn't matter which president and which year, because this kind of thing happens all the time. While he personally was remembering the resurrection of Jesus, others—Jews, Hindus, Muslims—were worshiping in different ways, and a shout out was directed their way as well. Jesus was placed up on the god shelf, along with all the others.

But if Jesus really did come back from the dead, then certain things are false, and the gigantic brotherhood of man has gone *pfft*.

The problem is not so much the secularists believing in the secularist religion—that much is to be expected, you know? The problem is when Christians fall for it in various ways. So let us keep our minds and hearts clear. Let us run through the options for those believers who hold that Jesus actually returned from the dead three days after His crucifixion. What does this mean? And by "options" I do not mean "legitimate options." Four out of those five options are fatal errors. The Lord is risen, and He has called us to follow Him. Follow Him where? What are the possible relations that this risen Christ could possibly have to the secular city? And which is the right one?[18]

1. *Christ the isolationist.* In this view, the world is going to Hell, and we are called to live in the lifeboat commune populated by those who know the ship is going down. The mentality that drives this is radically sectarian, which is why the lifeboats are usually pretty small, and getting smaller. Not infrequently, it ends with pure churches of one member each bobbing around on their individual inner tubes.

2. *Christ the conference grounds organizer.* Here the world is also going to Hell, but it will be a while yet, and we have to live the bulk of our lives out "there." So arrangements have been made for our restorative "getaways," and we periodically retreat to these conference grounds for talks that cheer us up before we have to go back out into the world, in order to live in the way that our masters out there tell us to.

3. *Christ the figurehead.* In this setup, Christ is given the preeminent place of honor, religiously speaking, but the

---

18 H. Richard Niebuhr, *Christ and Culture* (New York: Harper & Brothers, 1951). For the original and much more scholarly statement of these options, Niebuhr gave us *Christ Against Culture, Christ of Culture, Christ Above Culture, Christ and Culture in Paradox,* and *Christ the Transformer of Culture.*

fundamental rules by which the affairs of state are governed are the ancient ways of death. Dostoevsky gave us a little sketch of this system when Jesus was hauled before the grand inquisitor.

4. *Christ the imperial slave.* Empires are pragmatic and pretty easygoing. Any religious group numerous enough to constitute a constituency will be invited to participate in International Religious Awareness Week. Their amusement park ride "of faith" will be commended along with all the other rides, and the one rule is that the pluralistic state gets to set the ticket prices, organize everything, print the brochures, and take in the receipts.

5. *Christ the Lord.* This is the view set forth in the pages of the Scriptures. All authority has been given to Him, and we, the children of men, have to what He says. For starters, we begin with "repent and be baptized." We then move on to learning to do "everything He has commanded."

In our public square tangles, we have gotten ourselves into trouble as a result of believing what the nonbelievers tell us about our arrangement. Whenever Christians try to argue for "principled pluralism," they are doing so on the basis of this trust—and it is profoundly a misplaced trust.

Think of it this way. When a *Christian* says that Christians ought not to insist that Jesus be recognized as Lord in the public square, he is either saying that we shouldn't do this because Jesus doesn't want us to, or we shouldn't do this because Jesus doesn't care, making it OK for us to go along with the secular flow.

But if Jesus wants the public square to be secular, how did
we learn this? From the Bible? And if we arrange the public
square in this way because of what *Jesus* said, isn't this just
a form of theocracy? And if we go the other way and say
that Jesus doesn't care what goes on in the public square, and
we can therefore make a treaty with the secularists out there,
two questions arise. One, how do we know Jesus doesn't care?
Did He say? If He didn't, how do we know? If He did, then
isn't this just another theocracy variation? Two, supposing He
doesn't care, in what way does this make the secularists trust-
worthy? Suppose that we just somehow magically know that
Jesus doesn't mind us making treaties with the secularists in
and with regard to the public square. We still are up against
this next question, which is whether or not we should believe
what the secularists are promising to do. Who is *their* god?
Why should they keep their word? Is their word good? In
short, where is this secularism coming from?

Let us suppose that, instead of our abstract idols (represented by words like *neutrality*, *pluralism*, *democracy*, *secularism*, and so forth) the public square was governed by a giant
named Dimblemuffin, who lived in a castle on a hill overlooking our town. The giant drank too much, had a red nose,
and would eat some of the peasants from time to time, and
I use illustrations like this because I am trying to make ab-
struse political and theological issues accessible to the modern reader. Now suppose that we had Christian theologians
who maintained that it was crucial for us to limit the authority of Jesus Christ to the spiritual realm of the Church,

and Dimblemuffin could have the rest. In fact, Dimblemuffin needed to have the rest. And suppose further they added that to propose that Jesus be acknowledged as having authority over the whole shebang would actually be an insult to *Him*, and to the true spirituality of the Church. And, this being the *actual* point, it was also pointed out that to suggest altering our arrangement might make Dimblemuffin very, very angry.

In that setting, to go along would not only be compromise, it would be craven compromise. And that is what it remains even when we use the noble-sounding, conscience-easing words, not one of which has a red nose.

All the vexed political issues that we confront reduce to cultural options considered above, considered in relationship to Christ. But it is not always immediately obvious how that process works. For example, James Davison Hunter has given us a very thorough treatment of culture and how to change it. In it, he describes what actual cultural change looks like, and he gives us this description in eleven propositions. It is superb, not because these propositions cover everything, but rather because they reveal how much needs to be covered. I have a few *yeah, buts*, but I will get to those in a minute.

First is my summary of his eleven points, the last four having to do with the dynamics of cultural change.

1. Culture is a system of intertwined truth claims and moral obligations.

2. Culture is shaped over the course of history.

3. Culture is inherently dialectical, with that dialectic existing on two levels. The first is the dialectic between ideas

and institutions, and the second between individuals and institutions.

4. Culture is a resource and a form of power.

5. Culture is an entity that has both a center and a periphery.

6. Culture is generated by supportive networks for influential leaders.

7. Culture is not autonomous and is not fully coherent.

8. Cultures change from the top down, not from the bottom up.

9. Cultures change when second-string elites get dissatisfied.

10. Cultures change the most when the networks of elites and the institutions they lead overlap.

11. Cultures change, but not without a fight.[19]

My first caveat is something I am not yet sure whether Hunter would agree with or not. This would require an additional proposition or a significant expansion of his first one. It is striking to me that there is no mention of worship here. Culture is a religion's exoskeleton, and every culture is the external embodiment of some *cultus*, worship. Every culture has a worship center, and every worship center has an external cultural shape—or is a newcomer in the midst of challenging the current cultural shape that is the work of the other gods.

Truth claims and moral obligations, which Hunter rightly points to, arise out of worship and can arise in no other way. If there is no God, what is truth? If there is no God, there is no moral obligation. If there is a God, I bind myself to Him

---

19 James Davison Hunter, *To Change the World: The Irony, Tragedy, and Possibility of Christianity in the Late Modern World* (Oxford: Oxford University Press, 2010).

(*religio*) in worship. As the Breastplate has it, "I bind unto myself today, the strong name of the Trinity." It is clear that Hunter has a central place for the institutional Church, but I want worship as a verb in the present tense. Places where God was worshiped once have institutional influence because of it, but not indefinitely. What is it that overcomes the world? Is it not our faith? More on this later, no doubt.

A second point. Hunter says this: "The idea, suggested by James Dobson, that 'in one generation, you can change the whole culture' is nothing short of ludicrous."[20] I think that Hunter is not keeping a clear enough distinction between statements made for public consumption and a settled theology of cultural change. An activist mobilizes a crowd for a statewide election differently than an academic carefully parsing the history of the world. A sergeant giving his troops the raw business before they charge the machine gun is not going to sound very nuanced. "On the other hand . . ." Demagoguery is simply the wicked use of this reality—but it remains a reality for all that. Nehemiah tells his men that they were fighting for their God, their wives, their families, and their homes (Neh. 4:14), which could easily be represented as *rah, rah* simplistic, right?

This has struck me before when I have met men who were evangelical leaders and heavily engaged in the culture wars. Let us say I had been previously tempted to think they were superficial because of how they spoke in their press releases. But these men often have a very good understanding of the

20 Ibid., 45.

complexity of the situation they are in. All this is to say that
Hunter is right to point out how complex cultures are. I just
want to add here that being a cultural activist is complex, too,
in other ways. And while there are rabble-rousers who only
know how to start a hubbub, there are also many thoughtful
men who know how complicated the challenges are. So if
they put out a brochure for a conference on "taking America
back," the chances are pretty good that they don't believe it
will be done with an election or two.

This leads to a discussion of a point Hunter makes, a point
that I believe to be a premature assessment: "As we have seen,
though, Christians have embraced strategies that are, by design,
incapable of bringing about the ends to which they aspire."[21]

To say this, ironically, Hunter has to accept the common
understanding of the life cycle of political and cultural change.
If it goes from election to election, or from one generation
to the very next one, then enough time has gone by to pronounce the Christian cultural engagement that began in the
seventies a failure. But what if the life cycle of real transformation is two hundred years? What if the agents of change
never really see the fruit of their labors? John Knox was one
of the great fathers of the American political arrangement,[22]
a fact that would have astonished him if you had attempted
to explain it to him.

I used the word *ironically* above because Hunter's central point in this section is that nearly everything has been

21 Ibid., 99.
22 Douglas Kelly, *The Emergence of Liberty in the Modern World* (Phillipsburg, NJ:
Presbyterian & Reformed, 1992).

politicized, a point which he makes very well. But I want to point out that Hunter has not noticed this very point when it comes to the definitions of cultural success and failure. In a highly politicized culture, you get to pronounce something a dud or a failure after the proponent of that dud or failure has been in office for more than several months and you are busy preparing *your* election bid. But yeast in the loaf doesn't obey the established election cycle. A nameless flayed martyr under Diocletian could not have anticipated Charlemagne—but was responsible for him nonetheless. A politicized culture lives on a small planet, so the horizon is always not that far away. But we actually live on a big planet.

So in this discussion Hunter turns to consider the nature of political power and the relationship that Christians do have and should have to that power. Everyone recognizes that, at the end of the day, power and force are necessary to keep a society from fragmenting. This becomes increasingly necessary as other cultural ties become frayed.

"The politicization of everything is an indirect measure of the loss of a common culture and, in turn, the competition among factions to dominate others on their own terms."[23] This is exactly what is happening to us; it is the way it is.

"What else is there to hold such a society together? What remains to bind together its innumerable fragments? The answer, in large part, is power–the exercise of coercion or the threat of its use."[24] This is a good description of fragmenting

---

23  Hunter, 107.
24  Ibid., 101.

cultures where the leaders find themselves having to knock heads every fifteen minutes, where contempt for the *moral* authority of that culture has largely eroded. No society can enforce its laws on everyone. In order for a culture to work, the vast majority of the compliance has to be genuinely voluntary, rendered out of love, loyalty, or affection. Coercion is applied to the outliers, for the benefit of those who were thinking about becoming outliers. Strike the fool, and the simple learn wisdom. But if the entire populace is made up of simpletons and fools, at some point they will storm the castle.

A society that is under the blessing of God, that is not experiencing what René Girard called a "sacrificial crisis,"[25] is a society that is held together by amity and loyalty. Force is necessary, but it is not the central glue. When it becomes the central glue—and I think Hunter is dead right about his observations on this concerning our culture—that is a sign of real trouble.

As noted earlier, Hunter is right to describe contemporary society as one in which there is a "tendency toward the politicization of nearly everything."[26] But he makes a significant misstep, and the emphasis following is mine.

> Slowly, often imperceptively, there has been a turn toward law and politics as the primary way of understanding all aspects of collective life . . . *The tendency now effects* [sic] *conservatives every bit as much as it does liberals; those*

---

25  Girard, *Violence and the Sacred* (Baltimore, MD: Johns Hopkins, 1977), Chapter Two.

26  Ibid., 102.

*who favor small government as it does those who want a larger government.* It has affected everyone's language, imagination, and expectations, not least conservatives who, like others, look to law, policy, and political process as the structure and resolution to their concerns and grievances; who look to politics as the framework of self-validation and self-understanding and ideology as the framework for understanding others.[27]

For the moment, let us leave out of our discussion compassionate conservatism, big-government conservatism, bombs-away conservatism, telegenic conservatism, and other forms of nonconservative conservatism. When we see ambitious head representatives of these kinds of conservatism debate with the lefties on television over their issues, the question really is over whether the nanny state should make us all wear red T-shirts or blue T-shirts. I would have no trouble if Hunter wanted to tag opportunists like that with the sin of accommodating themselves to the politicization of nearly everything. That point is not only true, but also needs to be made over and over again. Such patheticos calling themselves conservatives are a public nuisance, and kudos to anybody willing to pitch in to help clean up that mess.

But Hunter explicitly does *not* do that. He tags genuine conservatives, those "who favor small government," and he says they are affected "every bit as much" as are the advocates of a government that got itself all swoll up.

27  Ibid., 108.

Think about this for a minute. Principled opponents of the politicization of everything are part of the politicization of everything? But a genuine conservative, who wants the federal government to be one-fifth the size it currently is, cannot be a partaker of the politicization of everything. If the government were that size, they would run out of money in mid-February, and everybody would live nonpoliticized lives until the following January. The word we used to use to describe that state of affairs, kids, was *liberty*. Get your great-grandfather to tell you stories about it sometime.

A hyperpoliticized climate *is* one of the central challenges we face. But Hunter, after helpfully pointing this out, wants to say that there is no difference between Obama over there, riding the dragon while waving his cowboy hat, and St. George down here, trying to kill the dragon with a lance in order that a forlorn Obama might have a carcass to sit on. It is quite true to say that both are *occupied* with the dragon, but to stop there is to miss the central point of what is happening. One is riding it and the other is fighting it, trying to kill it.

Put simply, small government conservatives are fighting the hyperpoliticization of everything, and that is explicitly and precisely what they are fighting, as they have patiently and repeatedly explained all along. Now in order to fight something like that it is necessary to go over and stand near it. To retreat to an ivy-covered office in the academy in order to write about faithful presence and, in the process, to construct a mash-up of conservatives and liberals who are "both being too close to the dragon" is, it seems to me, to miss a central point in a quite striking way.

Also important for any discussion of Christian culture-changing is the relationship of the authority of the Church to the authority of the civil magistrate, of which there are three basic varieties. The first is the route taken by ultramontane Jesuits (not to mention some ultramontane Presbyterians), in which scheme the final authority is held by the Church, with the pope at the head of it. The second is that of Erastianism, where it is taught that the state has final and supreme authority over the Church. The third is that of Kuyperian sphere sovereignty, where the different spheres function according to the law of Christ, only answering to one another in those areas where Scripture teaches that their concerns overlap. There are, of course, variations within each party, with different people leaning this way or that, or reacting to the other thing.

But those are the basic options—the state gives way to the Church, the Church gives way to the state, or the Church and state figure out where their respective boundaries are.

In arguing for mere Christendom, it would be an easy mistake for some to assume that this necessitates a Protestant form of the first option—some kind of ecclesiocracy. But, in fact, I want to argue that the historic Reformed position is a variation of the third option—a Kuyperian settlement of some sort. But in describing this above, I mentioned that both sides had figured out where the boundaries are, which is trickier than it looks.

I should make another side comment first. These different options can be supported in different ways. For example,
a person could argue for the Church having authority over
all others because that is the way he has the flow chart set
up, or he could urge a system whereby the competitors have,
in the Marxist sense, "withered away." The former would be
seen with a strong medieval pope and surly princes, while the
latter would be seen in an anabaptist eschatology, where the
Church wins the demolition derby of history and is the last
vehicle running. For my purposes here, whether it is represented eschatologically or not, it mattereth not.

I want to make two points about all this, one historical and
the other . . . not.

The first is that the historic Reformed position is the
Kuyperian one, even before Kuyper, and that the current attempts to radically separate these spheres is radically uncon-
fessional. There will be more on this in a subsequent chapter,
but for now, Calvin and numerous other Reformers would
have found the modern accommodations astonishing. Let's
hear what the gentlemen who wrote the Westminster Confession thought about it:

> The civil magistrate may *not* assume to himself the ad-
> ministration of the Word and sacraments, or the power
> of the keys of the kingdom of heaven: yet *he hath author-*
> *ity*, and it is his duty, to take order that unity and peace
> be preserved in the Church, that the truth of God be
> kept pure and entire, that all blasphemies and heresies
> be suppressed, all corruptions and abuses in worship and

discipline prevented or reformed, and all the ordinances of God duly settled, administered, and observed. For the better effecting whereof, he hath power to call synods, to be present at them *and to provide that whatsoever is transacted in them be according to the mind of God.*[28]

They begin by denying the raw Erastian option—where the civil magistrate is told that he may not administer the Word and sacraments, and he does not hold the power of church discipline. The president may not, in short, preach the gospel, administer the Lord's Supper, or intrude himself into matters of church discipline. That is what he may not do. What may he do? He can keep the peace in the Church, keep the truth from getting fragmented, suppress blasphemy and heresy, enforce the patterns of biblical worship, and see to it that the ordinances of God are kept. In order to enable him to do this, he can call synods of the Church, he can be present at them, and he can ensure that the churchmen stick closer to the text than they might want to. Anybody have the willies yet?

This section of Westminster was modified by the American Presbyterians in the downgrade of 1789:

Civil magistrates may not assume to themselves the administration of the Word and sacraments; or the power of the keys of the kingdom of heaven; or, *in the least*, interfere in matters of faith. Yet, *as nursing fathers*, it is the *duty* of civil magistrates *to protect the Church of our common Lord*, without giving the preference to any denomination of *Christians* above the rest, in such a man-

28 Westminster Confession of Faith 23.3, emphasis mine.

ner that all ecclesiastical persons whatever shall enjoy the full, free, and unquestioned liberty of discharging every part of their sacred functions, without violence or danger. And, as Jesus Christ hath appointed a regular government and discipline in his Church, no law of any commonwealth should interfere with, let, or hinder, the due exercise thereof, among the voluntary members of any denomination of *Christians*, according to their own profession and belief. It is the duty of civil magistrates to protect the person and good name of all their people, in such an effectual manner as that no person be suffered, either upon pretence of religion or of infidelity, to offer any indignity, violence, abuse, or injury to any other person whatsoever: and to take order, that all religious and ecclesiastical assemblies be held without molestation or disturbance.[29]

Both forms of the Confession acknowledge that the magistrate has authority *circa sacra*, around sacred things, and both deny that he has authority *in sacris*, in sacred things. I want to argue that both are basically Kuyperian, although they are obviously leaning in different directions. We might struggle with the original Confession, where it says that the magistrate has the authority to determine that decisions by Church synods are in conformity with the Word of God. How is that not taking away with an Erastian hand what was given to the Church earlier in the paragraph with a Kuyperian hand? That is a reasonable question. But we should also have trouble with the American version, where it says that the magistrate

---

29  Westminster Confession of Faith 23.3, emphases mine.

cannot interfere with matters of faith "in the least." How is this not sowing the seeds of a later departure of the civil magistrate from any duty to Christ whatever?

But, in fact, both forms of the Confession are *assuming* a continued Christian predominance in civil society, a predominance which did not in fact occur. The British Westminster wanted one denomination of Christians to be selected as the Church of England. The Americans wanted the government (at every level) to refuse to play favorites among *Christian* denominations, but the American Presbyterians wanted the magistrate to do this *as Isaiah's nursing father*, protecting the Church of "our common Lord." To the extent that Buddhists and Muslims entered their thinking (hardly at all), they would not have wanted any citizen to be *persecuted* for their faith, but they would at the same time have wanted the civil magistrate to be protective in a special way of the Christian Church, made up of different denominations of Christians. The British version of Westminster is a variation on the older form of Christendom. The American form is much closer to what I am calling mere Christendom.

It is common for people to think, when the original Reformed views of the civil magistrate are brought up, that the American revision fixed "all that." They certainly moderated it, but did so in the conviction that they were describing the magistrate's relationship to a *Christian* country. Once the pagans and unbelievers arrived *en masse*, we are back to the problems that Constantine faced.

Here is the other thought, of a more devotional nature. Party spirit and factionalism can afflict spheres as well as Whigs and Tories, or Methodists and Baptists. This has happened numerous times in history. God has created three basic spheres—the family, the Church, and the civil order. These were all created directly by God and not by man.

Now humility delights in the prerogatives given to *another*, and hubris insists that, in the final analysis, things are going to have to go the way of me and my faction. To want the Church to supplant the family and state is just as bad as wanting the state to supplant the Church and family. There are times when eschatology reveals not the faith of Abraham, but the conceits of Diotrophes. We push our way to the front of the disciples and ask if *we* can sit at the Lord's right hand when He comes into His kingdom. It is amazing that after two millennia we are still flunking that particular test. We are still arguing on the road, as we walk behind Him.

Kuyperianism is the only option presented to us that guards against the hubris that is always wanting to float up to the surface of our hearts in whatever sphere we happen to be. As a minister of the Church, I am to delight in the fact that in the kingdom there will be kings and princes way ahead of me. And that is not as easy as it looks.

# 3

# ISLAMISM

Wʜen defenders of the Western secular system point out the threat of sharia law and the encroachments of Islamic fundamentalism, they are right to do so. But the way it usually goes is unfortunate, because the ground where they want to stand in this fight is ground that gives way under their feet. Sharia law is "abhorrent to Western values." So? Who cares about that?

The rise of Islamic fundamentalism is complicated subject driven by various insecurities over the success of the "Christian" West, the attempts of their own leaders to accommodate the West, grinding poverty in the countries that Allah is supposed to be blessing, and so on. But at the center, the Islamists are driven by what Allah has *revealed*. The answer to this is not what the people of the West think at the present moment. If you want a good example of the voice of *that* god, then take a gander at the House of Representatives. A transcendental appeal, even if it might be false, appears to outrank a horizontal appeal that is known by everyone to be false.

Here is the basic problem. Why should we resist the encroachments of sharia law based on our Western values? What is the opposite of Western values? That would be Eastern values, and can anybody give me a reason why we should prefer one position over another on the basis of *geography*?

Western values have value only if they are a coded way of referring to something else. And that something else cannot be another horizontal fact, like representative government, or women's rights, or anything like that. That just pushes the question back a step. Why should we prefer those? And if we say that Western values simply means "our values," then why should those outrank "their values"? In the ebb and flow of Darwinian struggle, *ours* sometimes loses to *theirs*.

"Western values" as an appeal works only if it is a coded reference to Christendom, and that only works if Christ is still there. Anything else is arbitrary, jingoistic, and stupid. Anything else is a couple of dogs fighting over a piece of meat. Right now, we are the bigger dog—but we are also a bigger dog in the middle of some kind of existential crisis.

The problem is illustrated by secular or atheistic Zionism, which is racism, straight up. If you make a *theological* argument for Jews in the land of Palestine, that argument is based in the will of God and not in the inherent right of a certain DNA imprint to hold the rights to a certain bit of territory. Even if that theological argument is wrong, the appeal it makes is not to race (Deut. 7:7–8). But if there is no God, and hence no theological argument, all you have left of your Zionism is race. "I can have this, and you cannot have it, because I am a Jew, and you are not." Zionism of that sort, Zionism with no God, is racism pure and simple. Of course, if there is no God, there is nothing wrong with such racism, and nothing wrong with answering it in kind, but that is another point for another day.

In a similar way, Western values are a bundle of wind, a bunch of nothing. The postmodernists have pointed out to us that there are different communities out there, and they all have their values, and so now these communities careen around in our global village like so many bumper cars. Who's to say?

Western values are to be preferred in a conflict like this only if they are grounded in some way in the will of God. If they are not, then they will go down before the will of Allah like dry grass before the scythe. Islamism will go through deracinated Western values like a hot knife through butter. It goes back to Chesterton's adage—if you don't stand for something you will fall for anything.

Now there have been times, times of unreflecting youth, when a people with their false little democratic gods on a shelf might successfully stand against another people with their false Allah-god up in the air. Sometimes Jupiter prevails over Mithra, and sometimes it goes the other way. That kind of thing has been done, and it has actually been done by the people of the West to the Muslims. Think of the Western democracies of the early twentieth century carving up the Middle East like it was a pie. Yes, it has been done.

But that was before the rot of postmodernism set in, the *reductio* that made all our crackerjack thinkers realize (some of them reluctantly) that our great Kantian sky hook wasn't actually *bolted* to anything, and one man's guess was as good as another's.

So this means, in short, that there is now no way to defend the West without rejecting, root and branch, the last one hundred years of Western intellectual history. That's fine with me, and all my modest proposal entails is that we undertake to defend the West by rejecting the last two hundred and fifty years of Western intellectual history. I am willing to defend the next Christendom, and am in fact eager to do so. I am not willing to take my stand on the basis of the dregs of the former Christendom.

So when I speak of secularism cratering, I am referring to official, state-sponsored agnosticism cratering. I am not referring to any coming obliteration of the necessary distinctions between the Church and the world, between the Church of Christ and the Kingdom of God.

So let us begin there. The Church should think of the entire world as her parish. It is out in the parish that people grow barley, repair automobile engines, cut flowers, make love, and, despite the late sixties, make war. The Church is the ministry of Word and sacrament. Theocracy is necessary and inescapable. Ecclesiocracy is, among other things, quite an appalling thought. I understand that for many moderns those two terms are interchangeable, and that is one of the reasons we are in the difficulties we are in. When the parishioners come to church, they are taught and instructed in their duties of discipleship, and they are fed and nourished so that they might have the strength to meet these duties. There is a very real sense in which these members of the Church go out into the world as representatives of the Church, bringing the Church with them. But it is also true that they come into the Church as representatives of the world, bringing the world with them. Not the *worldliness* of the world, but certainly the earthiness of the world. And this materiality includes what the kings bring with them—honor and glory, about which more later.

Godless secularism still maintains an impressive facade. Like an ornate shell of a long-dead creature of the deep blue sea, there is enough to keep quite a number of people from pointing out the obvious, to wit, that the shell is hollow. A lot of people have also conspired together to not notice what is going on. The reasons for this conspiracy can be summed up in one word, which is "paycheck." But there are reasons for believing this cannot be kept up for much longer.

But while many are refusing to acknowledge the obvious, there is a large group of people who do see that the internal faith that used to sustain the West is now completely gone from the central corridors of power, and that their false certainties will always trump that benign and agnostic shrug of the shoulder. The Muslims are coming after the values of our hollow secularism, and watching it is not like watching an *actual* contest—it is like watching someone take a jackhammer to a soufflé.

The strength still manifested by the West is all residual or borrowed. The residue is left over from previous generations when men were more faithful, and the shell, while hollow, still had some strength. The borrowed is taken from the red state enclaves. That game cannot be kept up much longer.

Some secularists want to laugh off the Muslims—pointing at the state of plumbing in places like Somalia. But contests like this are not determined by counting the guns. You cannot decide a war by comparing the relative size of the GDP. Who was stronger, the Roman Empire or the barbarians who overran it? Wars are not tautological—the stronger force is not whichever wins by definition. Who was stronger? Boris Yeltsin holed up in his house or the Soviet Union with all its nukes? History is littered with examples of empires, nations, and cities that fell to inferior forces when by all rights they should not have.

Secularism is a spent force. Its inconsistencies are on display for all to see, and anyone not actively involved in taking bribes should be willing to say so.

The reaction to the proposed Ground Zero mosque a few years back provided us with a wonderful case study of public square issues and of the great need for a new Christendom. And since the opportunities in this situation to gain wisdom are enormous, it is not surprising that just about everybody is refusing to do so.

Hugh Hewitt is a responsible conservative commentator, and he does a lot of good work. But, in common with many public thinkers today, he missed this key point.

Here is an example of why my concerns (expressed repeatedly) about American exceptionalism and Christian refus-
als to acknowledge Christ in the public square are not concerns about a bundle of nothing. In his comments explaining
why he opposed the building of the Cordoba Mosque near
Ground Zero,[30] Hewitt said some things that make it obvious
why the apostle John had to warn Christians to keep themselves from idols (1 Jn. 5:21). John had to warn us because it
is a thing that Christians might not want to avoid.

Hewitt said that he did "not believe the Ground Zero
mosque should be built." The emphasis following is mine.

> I oppose it because the land and buildings damaged by
> the assault are now *part of the sacred space of America's
> great civic religion.* I would oppose the construction of
> *any sectarian project* there that wasn't a rebuild of an ex-
> isting *sectarian use* for the same reason. There is no for-
> mal designation for *the sacred spaces of America's civic re-
> ligion* though they extend from the Mall to the Arizona
> Memorial. The land around Ground Zero is very much
> part of that space, and any project that politicizes it *or
> brings a religious purpose to those sites* should be refused.[31]

There are three basic problems here, and they are really *basic* problems.

---

30  As an aside, before proceeding to the argument, for those who don't know,
*cordoba* is a Middle Eastern word meaning "here's a burnt stick in your eye."

31  Hugh Hewitt, "The Ground Zero Mosque: Why or Why Not?", *Hugh
Hewitt,* August 3, 2010, http://www.hughhewitt.com/the-ground-zero-mosque-
why-or-why-not/ (accessed Sept. 2016).

The first is that a conservative Christian is using words and phrases like *sacred space* and *religion*, without scare quotes, in order to describe spaces and a religion that are not Christian. And he is not describing them as sacred to the use and understanding of others, but sacred to us, as Americans. This means that he is saying that American Christians can lawfully belong to two religions, one civil and one up in the sky somehow. American Christians can worship in two different kinds of sacred spaces, one in which God is triune, and in the other where He isn't anything of the kind. It also means that patriotic Americans who are not Christian have an area of "worship overlap" with those who are Christian. We share sacred space, as sacred space, with people who don't love Jesus. The question really ought to arise—how did we get *here*?

This is the sort of thing that gives theologians like Yoder plausibility. This is the kind of thing of that makes you want to cite Yoda about the dangers of Constantinianism. "Once you start down the dark path, forever will it dominate your destiny, consume you it will." Yoda, Yoder, whatever. This is the kind of political analysis that a freshman in the Eusebian School of Panegyrics might have written for his first homework assignment, late in the evening and after a couple of beers.

The second problem is that to recenter America's public space like this means that manifestations of the Christian faith become "sectarian" with reference to it. And this is precisely how Hewitt argues. This mosque and Tim Keller's church in Manhattan are both "sectarian" in reference to this new sacred space. The fact that one does not worship the true

God and the other does is irrelevant to this relativization. This space is now sacred because it is the place where some terrorists blew themselves to Hell, and so ministers of the gospel of Jesus Christ must consider themselves to be outside that Established Church. All Christians, who worship the God who made Heaven and Earth, and who worship God through His true and only Son, are placed by a *Christian* political thinker on the same footing as Melanesian frog worshipers. We, and they, are Dissenters when it comes to this American sacred space. Well, we are Dissenters only if we dissent—which consistent Christians must do.

The third problem is that no idolatry can be internally self-consistent, and so a weird contradiction appears immediately. Hewitt objects to any project that "politicizes" this sacred space, but all we have are politics now. The sacred space was formed by a political terrorist act, and it was defended by those who were defending a particular political order. How can we object to the politicization of politics? This is all happening in the earthly city, in the *polis*. If this *polis* is being lifted up above the roil and rack of earthly commotions, then it has to be done arbitrarily, like the apotheosis of some dying Caesar, coughing up blood. Even Vespasian knew better than this with his famous last words—*Vae, puto deus fio*. "Dear me, I must be turning into a god . . ."

Nature is not the only thing that abhors a vacuum. Religion abhors a vacuum. If you banish all religious trappings from the public square, all you have done is swept and garnished the room in preparation for the new, sevenfold religion that is now on your doorstep, and with some creepy music playing in the background. And this is why exorcists who have no gospel are just an advance team for more demons. This is why Christian theologians who want to radically separate the two kingdoms are not doing what they *think* they are doing.

God has placed eternity in our hearts, and we behave like religious beings (because we must) wherever we go, and whatever we do. This is why Christian ministers must proclaim the crown rights of King Jesus everywhere, and over everything. All authority in Heaven and on Earth has been given to Him, and this means that Jesus Christ owns Lower Manhattan, having purchased it with His precious blood. No other blood can be allowed to trump this, or compete with it, not even the blood of courageous firemen. We cannot give "this part" to Jesus and the remainder to nobody in particular, or to Mr. Neutrality. All attempts to "divvy up" are simply negotiations with idols. But we are Christians and are not allowed to parlay with idols.

Given what has gone before, Hugh Hewitt is simply being consistent in his use of words like *sacred* and *religious*. But it is a consistency we must turn back from. In order to do this, we have to reject Americanism, an *ism* every bit as ugly as all the other isms out there. I give way to no one in my love for my country, my nation, and my people. But it is a *nation*, for pity's sake, not a god. It is a *country*, a fine place to shoot off firecrackers and eat hot dogs on the Fourth. But if you want me to trot out divine honors along with the flag, then my response will be a thoroughly American one. "What, are you *nuts*?"

We can try to understand our circumstances by flipping the whole thing with radical Islam around. Suppose that an American daisy-cutter bomb had been dropped on Mecca, and blew up their sacred rock. Suppose further that through a series of circumstances, a Southern Baptist gentleman proposed building a Christian chapel on the lip of that crater. We would be justified in supposing this man to be any number of things, but one of the things he emphatically would *not* be is a moderate.

The fact that he would not be a moderate would not make him a terrorist, of course. It would just make him *not a moderate*. He would be doing something provocative, and he would be doing it on purpose. If he denied being provocative, this would simply make him a dishonest nonmoderate. A real moderate would have stayed home.

Our secularists tend not to see this because they have made the fatal mistake of believing their own propaganda. All religious differences, they think, are mere denominational differences, and they are prepared to unbend liberally when it comes to such denominational distinctives, considered as such. They say, for example, that a free country should allow their Christians to debate whether to baptize with heads upstream or downstream. And then, with a patronizing pat on the head, we are sent on our way in order to debate how many angels our faith community thinks could fit on the head of a pin.

Religion, to them, is false, irrelevant, and pie-in-the-skyish. That being the case, they will treat forays by believers *as believers* into the political realm as blasphemous outrage, or as impossible contradiction. As a general rule of thumb, it is an outrage when Christians do it, and impossible when Muslims do it.

But on the eve of the Spanish Armada, a Roman Catholic Englishman could not be simply treated as one who believed in Purgatory, for example. Being a Catholic in that setting was a political act. When John of Leiden ascended to the throne of David in the Munster rebellion, to be an Anabaptist within a fifty mile radius was a political act. We think that different churches are all listed in the yellow pages so that we can know what time their services are, and that's it. But it is anachronistic to impose that mentality on those periods of (most of) history when politics and religion mingled in public together. The two cannot really be separated.

The rise of the secularist heresy and the voluntary quiescence of Christians in the West created an optical illusion. It *looked* like politics and religion were separated, when what had actually happened was that secularism established her religion, but with a stripped down liturgy and creed so that people would believe that it was somehow areligious. "Perhaps if we call it secular, then people won't notice how pervasively religious it is."

This technique was brazen, and it is the kind of thing that can sometimes work . . . for a time. It is like Christians calling their churches "nondenominational." But Grace Chapel, a designated nondenominational place of worship, is also, as it turns out, denominated (*named*) Grace Chapel. Abraham

Lincoln once asked how many legs a sheep would have if we call the tail a leg. Five, the answer came back. No, he replied, calling the tail a leg doesn't make it a leg. Calling it secular doesn't make it secular.[32]

Secularism pretended for a time to be neutral about the basic religious concerns, and it was actually anything but neutral. Creating a religion of man is not the same thing as abandoning religion. So after a time, the pretension wears thin, the contradictions start working their way to the surface, the old alliances and treaties are violated, and the old immanent gods no longer answer when we cry out in their temples.

This is why it is a political act to be a Muslim in America today. To be a Christian in America today is also *a political act*. It cannot be depoliticized by any ecclesiastical wish or theological whim. Meredith Kline has no wand to wave that will make any faithful Christians fit into this collapsing secular order. This is because our secularist overlords have lost their faith in the ghosts of Jefferson and Voltaire, and they have also lost the doctrinal rigor of their convictions and are wobbling along as best they can. In this crisis of secularist confidence, *to be a Christian at all is a political act of defiance.* The same goes for the Muslims—because secularist idols can be challenged by other idols, as well as by the true God. The Muslims, however, have been quicker to see the situation and quicker to exploit it than have Christians.

---

32  The response might be, to the objections to the Ground Zero mosque, that the sponsoring Muslims were liberals, not radicals. But what would we say if the Christian group wanting to build on the lip of the Mecca crater was a liberal one? Would it matter?

If the secularist state could somehow continue on, unruf-
fled, for the next three centuries, a lot of Christians could
continue on with their compromises with it. Sure. And if the
sky fell, we would all catch larks.

But that is not our situation. Bricks are already falling out
of their wall. Their towers are already swaying back and forth.
The corrosive acids of their relativism have eaten away all the
strength of their three-hundred-year-old mortar. Many of us
do not yet see this. So? When the walls of Jericho fell down,
I dare say that there were more than few Israelites who were
caught flat-footed. But ready or not, here we come.

The "hallowed ground" meme, not surprisingly, caught on.
Opponents of the mosque picked up the thread, urging the
construction of the mosque to be stopped and on that basis.
Supporters of the mosque, like the president, granted the le-
gitimacy of the point, but urged *their* denominational distinc-
tives about what is actually permissible on hallowed ground.
During the controversy, President Obama said that "Ground
Zero is, indeed, hallowed ground." But . . .

Since it is necessary for a public space to be defined by
one religion, the president thinks that it should be *his* religion—which, in this case, is multicultural mush. He wanted
to say that we can achieve liberty and justice for all if only
we followed the one rule at the heart of every religion, Islam
included, which was to do unto others.

His religion is Americanism—ick, poo, a religion that wants
all the "sectarian" faiths to take their place on the god shelf and
adopt as their central belief whatever the president says their

core values ought to be. But in the case of the Christian faith, the heart is *not* the Golden Rule—the heart of Christian ethics, sure, but ethics is not the gospel. Christ crucified, buried, and risen—that's the rule at the heart of our faith. Not only is it the center of our faith, it is a center that *cannot, by any means, be made to fit* on the rickety god shelf of the secularists.

But opponents of the mosque, like Charles Krauthammer, were in no better shape. He argued against the mosque, and his argument necessarily failed.[33] If you read through Krauthammer's article, you may have noted that he does make sense in a lot of ways, as he usually does. But this case has to be made, if it can be made, on the basis of something other than false theological claims, and Krauthammer pours a foundation of false theological claims, and does so in his first paragraph: "A place is made sacred by a widespread belief that it was visited by the miraculous or the transcendent (Lourdes, the Temple Mount), by the presence there once of great nobility and sacrifice (Gettysburg), or by the blood of martyrs and the indescribable suffering of the innocent (Auschwitz)."

But if a place can be made hallowed by "a widespread belief," then Mecca is as sacred as Ground Zero. In fact, it is more sacred than Ground Zero because a "widespread belief" about a false transcendent faith is going to necessarily displace a "widespread belief" about a false immanent faith. Despite his not existing, Allah still outranks the pushmi-pullyu Baals of consumerism and entertainment. *If this is all we have,* rape

33 Charles Krauthammer, "Sacrilege at Ground Zero," *National Review*, August 13, 2010, http://www.nationalreview.com/article/243668/sacrilege-ground-zero-charles-krauthammer (accessed Sept. 7, 2016).

outranks masturbation. In order to answer the transcendental claims of the Koran, we need to appeal to the transcendental *truth*. It is not until we put Allah and the Lord Jesus
Christ side by side that the one that actually doesn't exist will
then appear at a disadvantage. Until then, if we are forced to
choose between an idolatry that knows what it believes and
an idolatry that is never quite sure, the latter will always give
way to the former.

In the meantime, instead of *hallowed* and *sacred* and so on,
we should just recognize the long-standing "fighting words"
limit on freedom of speech. In a 1942 decision, the Supreme
Court decided (9–0) that freedom of speech did not include
the right to stand on the sidewalk outside the funeral of
somebody's mom in order to taunt the mourners. That is a
disturbance of the peace, and if somebody tries it, the magistrate has every right to come and sit on his head. But in order
to prohibit "fighting words," it is not necessary to maintain,
as a point of law, that the deceased woman was *hallowed*, or
*sacred*, and that the taunter is guilty of blasphemy or sacrilege.
No, he is just being a jerk.

But even here, in order to tell the difference between just
and unjust fighting words, we need to have an orientating
faith, and this is something that secularism simply cannot
provide. The secularists cannot tell the difference between
gracious abortion protesters, full of love, and homo-bashers
like Fred Phelps, full of hate. After all, the secularist says,
reasoning closely, are they not both standing on a *sidewalk*?
Hmmm? Are they not both "*saying* stuff"?

The Muslims involved in this knew exactly what they were doing. Those who defended the construction of the mosque said that these were moderate Muslims, and are not to be lumped in with the terrorists. But think about it for a minute. There were reasonable questions to be asked about where the money for the mosque was coming from and what the imam there thought of Hamas and so on. But we didn't need to ask and answer those questions in order to determine whether or not he was a moderate. Of course he was not moderate—he was playing brinksmanship at Ground Zero. If he were really moderate, we never would have heard of him. He may not have been an immoderate fundamentalist, but he most certainly was an immoderate *something*.

And Muslims generally know what they are doing—in the Ground Zero battle and ongoing efforts like it. What is that exactly? They are exposing the intellectual, theological, and ethical bankruptcy of secularism, and they are doing it *on purpose*. To answer their challenge, someone as intelligent as Charles Krauthammer is reduced to saying that sacrilege is defined by what lots of people think, true or false doesn't matter, or where lots of people died, right or wrong doesn't matter either.

Someone really does need to tell secularist America that her gods are genuinely pathetic. And currently, the Muslims are doing this because the Christians won't. And the Christians who won't do this are not so much in need of a different kind of theology as they are in need of a different kind of spine.

# 4

# THE RADICAL BUG OUT

Any discussion of Christian politics will have to deal with a distinct alternative position which has claimed the name "Christian" and which is popular among certain liberals and modern academics, that of the Anabaptist tradition. We'll describe it quickly. In the introduction to *Calvin and the Anabaptist Radicals*, William Balke says two important things—important, that is, to the point I would like to make here.

The first is that the name *anabaptist* results in a classic example of misdirection. "The name 'Anabaptist,' or 'rebaptizer,' picks out what actually was only an incidental teaching."[34] There are many baptists today who share the anabaptist rejection of infant baptism, but who are not anabaptistic at all

---

34  William Balke, *Calvin and the Anabaptist Radicals* (Grand Rapids, MI: Eerdmans, 1981), 11.

in their central assumptions. And, even more curiously, there are many today who call themselves confessionally Reformed who *do* buy into the central anabaptist assumption.

That central driving issue has to do with the way we relate the Church to the rest of human society outside the Church proper. In short, do you believe in the ideal of Christendom? If you do not, then you are historically anabaptist. If you are Calvinistic in your soteriology and historically Reformed in your ecclesiology, then you need to think Christendom is a good thing.

Balke notes, accurately, that "in the overall consciousness of the Western world, it [anabaptism] seems to have gained the victory."[35] This is why certain theologians, in the name of confessional Reformed orthodoxy no less, can attack advocates of Christendom as being heterodox and "suspect," *and get away with it.* If anabaptist assumptions had not carried the day, affecting virtually everybody who looks at Church–state issues, we would recognize this move as being as anachronistic as a picture of John Calvin in a Hard Rock Cafe Geneva T-shirt.

There's also a sort of neo-Anabaptism that is popular today, and, as is usually the case with neo's, it's more sophisticated and "subtle." James Davison Hunter says that this group, while not identical with original Anabaptism, nevertheless "keeps its distance from the State, maintaining a basic distrust toward its structure, action, and use of power."[36] It looks to the

---

35   Ibid., 9.

36   James Davison Hunter, *To Change the World: The Irony, Tragedy, and Possibility of Christianity in the Late Modern World* (Oxford, UK: Oxford University Press, 2010), 151.

primitive Church for its contrast of the Church and state, seizing on that point in history for a paradigm. Hunter notes, "[F]irst-century Christianity took form not only in a way that was independent of the State, but in a political environment that was hostile to the faith. This opposition was and remains centrally important to the Anbaptist identity and its vision of social and political engagement with the world."[37] Some of the names he treats here would include Stanley Hauerwas, John Yoder, and, downstream, some in the radical orthodoxy orbit, such as John Millbank and William Cavanaugh.

There are a few neo-Anabaptist statements recorded here by Hunter that require some comment. My first comment is one of enthusiastic agreement, although there will no doubt be some differences following hard after.

"As Hauerwas and Willimon put it, 'The church doesn't have a social strategy, the church *is* a social strategy.' The church does not have a social ethic, it is a social ethic."[38] This is absolutely correct, but this actually causes a real problem for the neo-Anabaptist project. The Church, over its history, has not *had* a Constantinian social strategy; the Church has *been* a Constantinian social strategy. Before the emperor converts, the Church simply is Constantinianism waiting to happen. After he converts, we of course have lots of bugs to work out. There will have to be more about this shortly.

Another observation would have been funny, had it not been so sad. "The commitment to nonviolence is paramount;

37  Ibid.
38  Ibid., 161.

the ethical mandate is always to resist coercion, whether from the state or the market."[39] Coercion from the market? But the market (rightly understood) is defined in terms of *non*coercion. If the assumption is that those markets are state-run or state-manipulated, then that is a real problem, but the problem is the state, not the market. But if the coercive power of the state is not involved in market transactions, and the market is free, then there is no coercion *by definition*—not unless you want to define Krispy Kreme running out of a man's very favorite variety ten minutes before he gets there as *coercion*. It might feel like coercion to him, I grant you, but it *isn't*.

Another comment was quite revealing on several levels. "But Jesus taught that his followers—or even the son of God!—should not attempt to 'run the world.'"[40] Right. That's the devil's job. It is the Church's job to sit off to the side in a lawn chair and nag, hector, fuss, and pick. Call it prophetic, and you can play it in such a way as to take no responsibility whatsoever. But why then do we pray for the kingdom to come, for His will to be done, on earth as it is in Heaven? I dunno. Just something we do.

One of the stretches where it is murky whether or not Hunter is summarizing their views or including his own *amens* can be found on mostly one page. Not surprisingly, the whipping boy is Constantine. Here you go. "Constantinianism was reinvented in the Reformation of the sixteenth century." "The error of Constantine was reinvented yet again in the age of

39   Ibid., 159.
40   Ibid., 159–160.

nationalism." "The archetype of the neo-Constantinianism was the founding of the American republic, where an informal establishment of Christianity became the basis of all the nation's governing institutions." The error shared by the Christian Right and Left is that they help perpetuate 'this ancient heresy.' "As the radical Orthodox theologians have helped to show, the Constantinian error now even extends . . . " [You get the drift. This is all said as though Constantinianism is a bad thing.] "The most egregious harm is done by conservative theologians—Protestant and Catholic—who continue to justify the Constantinian project."[41]

Another modern representative of the older Anabaptist view is Greg Boyd. The thesis of his book *The Myth of a Christian Nation* is this: "a significant segment of American evangelicalism is guilty of nationalistic and political idolatry."[42] If he had left it there, I would have had to agree, but he doesn't leave it there. *Why* are they guilty of this sin?

Boyd argues there is an unbridgeable chasm between the kingdom of God in the Church and the kingdom of the world, and that if they are in any way mingled or confused, the result will be spiritual disaster. As his subtitle puts it, the quest for political power is destroying the Church.

Jesus, according to Boyd, "never allowed himself to get pulled into the political disputes of his day."[43] And a driving

41  Ibid. The page in question is 154, except for the last one, which was, not surprisingly, 155.
42  Greg Boyd, *The Myth of a Christian Nation: How the Quest for Political Power Is Destroying the Church* (Grand Rapids, MI: Zondervan, 2006), 11.
43  Ibid., 11.

engine in this contemporary idolatry, according to Boyd, is the myth of a "Christian America" somewhere in our past. Boyd maintains, to the contrary, that "America is not now and never was a Christian nation."[44] The direct implication of what he is saying is also that it must never be a Christian nation in the future and that *Christians* should insist that it not ever become a Christian nation. "This nationalistic myth blinds us to the way in which our most basic and most cherished cultural assumptions are diametrically opposed to the kingdom way of life taught by Jesus and his disciples."[45]

But notice something here. Why is that bad? Is it *bad* for the kingdoms of the world to be diametrically opposed to the way of life taught by Jesus? The kingdoms of this world need to either *stop it* or they need to *carry on*. Boyd is arguing in this book that Christians must stop trying to get the kingdoms of this world to behave. But if no direction of any kind is forthcoming from the Church, then why can't the kingdoms of this world do whatever they want? This would presumably include aping the ways of the Church if it helps keep the populace docile. If they are diametrically opposed of *necessity*, then either I can head out to the commune or I can embrace living with the tension.

"Instead of providing the culture with a radically alternative way of life, we largely present it with a religious version of what it already is."[46] Comments like that sting, and for good

44  Ibid., 13.
45  Ibid.
46  Ibid.

reason. But given Boyd's assumptions, there is a *profound* confusion lying behind the comment. Boyd argues for a distorted two-kingdoms approach, and he does so with a vengeance. But his form of two-kingdom thought inevitably winds up in a tangled mess.

He starts out all right: "I'll suggest that the kingdom Jesus came to establish is 'not from this world' (John 18:36), for it operates differently than the governments of the world do."[47] And this: "Everything the church is about, I argue, hangs on preserving the radical uniqueness of this kingdom in contrast to the kingdom of the world."[48]

But here the confusion enters, naked and unashamed: "To insist that we keep the kingdom of God radically distinct from all versions of the kingdom of the world does not mean that our faith and moral convictions shouldn't inform our participation in the political process."[49]

In other words, the kingdoms of this world are an ugly camel, and will always be an ugly camel. Moreover, this dichotomy flattens the world outside the Church, meaning that all camels are more or less camels, and are more or less equally ugly. But Boyd allows that some Christians may want to entertain themselves come election time, some of them putting lipstick on the camel, while others opt for putting on some earrings. At some point, the more insightful among those who buy all the assumptions will slap their foreheads and

47  Ibid., 14.
48  Ibid.
49  Ibid., 15.

ask, "Why are we decorating the camels?" And they will then
move to Lancaster County, PA and buy a buggy.

The basic setup that Boyd argues for is this. God did not
*establish* civil governments, but rather "ordered" them to make
themselves not quite so bad as they otherwise would be. Fall-
en man had already come up with this way of dominating our
fellows, and God "ordered" it in such a way as to bring *some*
good out of it. When that good happens, we as Christians
should be thankful. And we should labor for justice within
the limits of this system, all while not holding our breath.
These are observations in a chapter where Boyd quotes a gentleman what has the last name of Yoder.

The reason we don't hold our breath is that while God man-
ages to restrain evil *somewhat* through the civil order, all civil
governments are in necessary degrees satanic, demonic, and
influenced by the god of this world, who is the devil. In short,
Boyd argues that nothing whatever can be done about this.
Not every civil government is equally bad at every moment,
but all civil governments are equally *compromised*, and therefore
we should invest ourselves in the kingdom of God. "But no
earthly kingdom, however good, is exempt from the scriptural
teaching that it is part of 'Babylon,' a worldwide kingdom ruled
by Satan."[50] If we have high hopes for the righteousness of the
civil order, those hopes are going to be dashed.

While he makes many shrewd observations in his book,
many of which folks in the religious right *do* need to hear, the
hinge of his whole argument is screwed into an astounding

50  Ibid. 21.

exegetical mistake—and it is not surprising that the door doesn't shut right at all.

Boyd says this: "Along these same lines, Jesus three times refers to Satan as the 'ruler of this world' (John 12:31; 14:30; 16:11). The term 'ruler' (*arche*) was a political term used to denote the highest ruling authority in a given region—and Jesus applied it to Satan over the whole world!"[51]

This just takes the breath away. Boyd is quite right about Satan, and *arche*, and the political implications of the term. But he ignores what the verses he cites are actually *saying*.

> Now is the judgment of this world: *now shall the prince of this world be cast out*. And I, if I be lifted up from the earth, will draw all *men* unto me. (Jn. 12:31–32)

> Hereafter I will not talk much with you: for the prince of this world cometh, *and hath nothing in me*. (Jn. 14:30)

> And when he is come, he will reprove the world of sin, and of righteousness, and of judgment: Of sin, because they believe not on me; Of righteousness, because I go to my Father, and ye see me no more; *Of judgment, because the prince of this world is judged*. (Jn. 16:8–11)

What Boyd does here is like writing a history of World War II and leaving out the stuff about Normandy. Jesus mentions Satan as an *arche*, all right, but He refers to him as a soon-to-be has-been *arche*. The kingdoms of this world have become the kingdoms of our God and of His Christ, and *He* shall reign forever and ever. The state of affairs that existed

51  Ibid., 21–22.

two thousand years ago certainly did exist in the way Boyd describes. Satan was the strong man. But Jesus came to bind the strong man . . . in order to take all his stuff. And he *did*.

Boyd mentions the fact that Satan had the authority to offer the kingdoms of the world to Christ when he tempted Him in the wilderness, which is quite true. And Christ refused, but not because it would be bad for Him to have them. He refused because He came as the conqueror—He came to *take* them, and would not receive them as a pretended gift.

I am not saying that Boyd is a Manichean, but it appears that he has a Manichean view *of history*. History is a static tug-of-war between good and evil, and nothing ever really changes. But in Scripture, Christ came, died, and rose again, and nothing can ever be the same. *There has been a turn in the tide of battle.* Christ humiliated the principalities and powers and made a public spectacle out of them. The kings of the earth, who used to be held in thrall by this *arche,* are now told to serve a different *arche*, the Lord Jesus Christ. They are told to kiss Him lest He be angry. They don't have to worry about the anger of their old master—*he* has been thrown down.

In times *past* God allowed the nations to walk in their own ways (Acts 14:16). That's not true anymore.

Before we can get very far in this business, we have to set aside a number of popular assumptions garnered from various hymns, sermons, and Far Side cartoons. The New Jerusalem is not a figure of Heaven, the final eternal state, but is rather a glorious image of the Christian Church. This is explicit in a number of places. The Jerusalem above, Paul says, is the mother of us all (Gal. 4:26). When we come to worship God on the Lord's Day, we do not come to an earthly mountain that can be touched (Heb. 12:18), but rather to a heavenly Zion (Heb. 12:22), a heavenly Jerusalem. And when the angel gives the invitation to John to come and see, the invitation is to see whom? The Bride, the wife of the Lamb (Rev. 21:2; 21:9–10). Who is that? Well, of course, the Bride of Christ is the Christian Church (Eph. 5:25). This city, made of transparent gold (Rev. 21:18), is a perfect cube. What else in the Bible is a perfect cube? The Holy of Holies in the Temple is that shape, and the Christian Church is explicitly described as the Temple of the Holy Spirit (1 Cor. 3:16–17; 6:19). So the New Jerusalem is the Christian Church, being gradually manifested through the course of history, gradually revealed in all her glory.

This should have obvious political implications. But first a word about how the glory of God works. The glory of God, when it visits the human race, does not obliterate us. The glory of God has infinite weight, but provided there has been propitiation, it does not crush–it lifts and exalts. Observe.

The New Jerusalem is described as *having the glory* of God (Rev. 21:11). The city does not require sun or moon, because the glory of *God* shines on it (Rev. 21:23). The city possesses the glory of the Almighty God Himself, and this glory is so resplendent that it makes the sun and moon superfluous. But, with the glory of sun and moon put in the shade, so to speak, what is *not* put in the shade?

"And the nations of them which are saved shall walk in the light of it: *and the kings of the earth do bring their glory and honour into it* . . . . And they shall bring *the glory and honour of the nations into it*" (Rev. 21:24, 26). The glory of God does not make the glory and honor of kings vanish. The glory of God does not make the glory and honor of the nations evaporate. This means that, within this image, while the glory of the sun and moon is dispensed with, the glory of kings and nations is *not*. Now this presupposes that the kings and nations are walking in the light of the glory of God in the Church, but doing this does not eradicate their glory, but rather *establishes* it.

There are those who believe that the civil orders of the nations have nothing good to commend them whatever, and that, once sin is dealt with, there will be nothing left worth speaking of. But the very next verse makes it clear that the sinfulness and corruption of our civil orders *has* been dealt with—specifically excluded is "any thing that defileth" (Rev. 21:27)—and yet kings and their honor and nations and their glory are not excluded, and they are glorious enough to be worthy of mention in this context.

So this means that Christians who labor now for the eradication of civil vice, folly, corruption, and tyranny—may their tribe increase—are working to shed a Zion light that the nations might enjoy. But when they have succeeded, they will not have achieved a Marxian "withering away" of the state, or some kind of an anarchist paradise. They will discover, rather, that they have established Solomonic majesty, true glory, and real honor.

If we were given a glimpse of these future rulers now, it would take the breath right out of us. If we were given just a glimpse of the livery of just their *servants*, there would be, as with the Queen of Sheba, no spirit left in us (1 Kgs. 10:5). And we would sit down in gladness, all our political questions answered.

The truth of the matter is that, come what may, we know that the one who will execute judgment upon sinners is the same one who suffered the penalty of God's wrath in place of sinners. We see that His heart is not one of malice, but rather of holiness. This means that when He executes "power over," there is nothing morally deficient about it. There is nothing suspect about it. It is righteous, holy, and good judgment. The problem is not that sinners are judged; the problem is that we *deserve* to be, and when it happens, there is no complaint department to sort things out afterward. Nothing will need to be sorted out afterward.

Boyd's problem here is that he takes certain passages, fixes them far off in the firmament, and then tries to read the remaining passages in the blinking starlight he has created.

"Though he rightfully should have been honored by the world's most esteemed dignitaries, he chose to fellowship with tax collectors, drunkards, prostitutes, and other socially unacceptable sinners."[52] Right. But Boyd left *centurions* off this list for some reason. And the omission is quite striking. Boyd spends a goodish bit of this chapter looking down his nose at those people who sacrifice themselves for Boyd's comfort, dismissing their sacrifices as mere power-grabbing. He

52  Ibid., 35.

simply assumes that motives in the "kingdom of the sword" must be corrupt, and cannot be pure the way motives in the Church can be pure. The policeman who stops a violent rapist is somehow participating in the "chain of hate."[53] Now Boyd has elsewhere acknowledged that God uses the civil magistrate to keep things tied together, but he is unwilling to acknowledge that Christians *serving as Christians* could be fully functioning as *faithful* servants of Christ in that role.

"If we follow the 'pattern of this world' (Rom. 12:2 NIV) and allow bitterness and hatred into our heart, and if we consequently demonize our enemy, we cannot possibly obey Jesus' teaching—or Peter's and Paul's."[54] "Where people choose violence, retaliation, and self-interest, however, they are merely participants in the kingdom of the world, however understandable or 'justified' their behavior is by kingdom-of-the-world standards."[55] The policeman who stops the rapist is "choosing violence, retaliation, and self-interest." It *happens* that the opposite of collateral damage—call it collateral edification, by accident—occurs, for which we thank God, but these instruments of His kindness (cops and soldiers) are fundamentally compromised. But suppose we have someone who bears the sword who has the *intention* of sacrificing himself for the sake of others.

Boyd says this: "The point is that love, through service, has a power to affect people in ways that 'power over' tactics do

53  Ibid., 41.
54  Ibid.
55  Ibid., 43–44.

not, and it is this unique power of self-sacrificial love that most centrally defines the kingdom of God."[56] But why does "power over" have to be about the person over whom the power is exercised? Why can't "love through service" be rendered to the people who are protected from the lawless? In short, this whole thing that Boyd sets up is a false alternative. There are selfish men bearing the sword, selfless men bearing the sword, selfish men not bearing the sword, and selfless men not bearing the sword.

But Boyd simply appeals to an NPR ethic, the kind of ethic that goes down smoothly with a five dollar latte. "When we respond to violence with violence, whether it be physical, verbal, or attitudinal, we legitimize the violence of our enemy and sink to his level."[57]

Boyd rejects an approach that is "practical and rational" as "power over" and inherently corrupted. To be practical and rational on a topic like crime control is to necessarily give way to self interest. "What is more, while the kingdom of the world is centered on what 'works' to achieve one's self-interests . . ."[58]

Boyd is nothing but an absolutist when it comes to his approach. "The *only* criteria that matters, then, in assessing whether anything has any value within the kingdom that God is building on the earth is love—love defined as Jesus dying on the cross for those who crucified him."[59] Boyd is right that the only thing that matters is love; his problem

56  Ibid., 38–39.
57  Ibid., 40.
58  Ibid., 43.
59  Ibid., 45.

comes with his "love defined as." Love is defined as Christ on the cross, a suitable blank screen for projecting all our accumulated sentimentalities. Yes, what matters fundamentally is love. But in the Bible love sometimes knocks heads together, fights serpents and dragons, silences the foe and the avenger, and casts the godless into Hell. Next time we say that to respond to violence with violence is tantamount to sinking to the criminal's level, and that we must not do this because of the character of *God*, then what are we to do about God responding to violence with violence?

Let us never forget that Hell is ultimate violence. It is certainly true that it formed no part of the uncreated and internal triune life, but it is a manifestation of God's holiness in *this* world. And we are supposed to think in terms of it and build our lives in accordance with that understanding.

Those who have a problem with the doctrine of Hell—sentimentalists all, and Rob Bell's teaching comes to mind—reject the teaching as troublesome, but then, because of their naïveté, set about creating hellish conditions here on earth. As my father has taught me, hard teaching creates soft-hearted people; soft teaching, which Boyd is serving up hot and gooey, right out of the oven, creates hard-hearted people. Sentimentalists are hard and brittle. Obedient Christians, accepting all that GOD has revealed to us, know that they are to be tenderhearted, forgiving one another, just as God in Christ forgave us.

But Boyd is not having any *tota et sola Scriptura*.

"The contrast is rather between two fundamentally different ways of doing life, two fundamentally different mindsets and belief systems, two fundamentally different loyalties."[60] So he wants ungodly people to do the dirty work of keeping people safe from harm. He wants the godly to withdraw into the cocoon of God's kingdom, where we might be *fully* cozy, wrapped up in the afghans of self-congratulation. Here *we* live, in the Church, following the way of sacrifice. We can see this at a glance in the fellowship hall, as we take another *koinonia* donut and cup of coffee. There *they* go, pursuing the cycle of hate, violence, and self-interest as they go out on patrol for another night, risking their lives so selfishly. Not like us Christians.

"The kingdom of the world trusts the power of the sword, while the kingdom of God trusts the power of the cross."[61] Actually, godly Christians trust in God in everything, and they utilize the appointed means for trusting Him in any given arena. Sometimes that is the sword, and sometimes it is turning the other cheek. Sometimes it is violence and other times it is the refusal to give way to violence. *It depends on what the Bible requires.*

"The kingdom of the world seeks to control behavior, while the kingdom of God seeks to transform lives from the inside out."[62] Sure. When the behavior is destructive, *somebody* needs to control it. This is one of the things that the Bible tells us to pray for, so that we might have the opportunity to present the gospel. Restraining people is not a final answer—of course not. But it is part of God's clearly revealed word. Our responsibility

60  Ibid., 46.
61  Ibid., 47.
62  Ibid.

is to stop spinning new kingdoms out of a prefab systematic theology and just receive what God has given.

Boyd strikes a wrong note when he quotes Bonhoeffer, who once said "Jesus concerns Himself hardly at all with the solution to worldly problems . . ."[63] Hardly at *all*? How could a mission to save the world not involve the solution of worldly problems?

It would be far better to say that Jesus came to solve *all* our worldly problems. The difference is that He does not do it the same way we do, which is to say, ineffectively. He really *will* save the world, and all our tin-pot messiahs won't. Salvation is only through Jesus, but it really is salvation that will be manifested in *this* world. Related to this, salvation from our worldly problems won't come from conservative armies or from liberal nannies.

Boyd rightly emphasizes that being a Christian involves imitation of Christ right at the center. "Thus, as disciples of Jesus we are to do what we see God doing in Jesus, just as our shadow does everything we do."[64] This is right—discipleship is imitation of Christ. So Boyd states the principle rightly, but then applies it wrongly. This discipleship "doesn't look like a group using swords, however righteous they believe their sword-wielding to be. It rather looks like people individually and collectively mimicking God. It looks like Calvary."[65]

All right then. Imitate *this*. "And out of his mouth goeth a sharp sword, that with it he should smite the nations: and

63  Ibid., 51.
64  Ibid.
65  Ibid., 52.

he shall rule them with a rod of iron: and he treadeth the winepress of the fierceness and wrath of Almighty God" (Rev. 19:15).

And we can't just hand this one over to Jesus to handle by Himself—because it contains a quotation from the second Psalm, which is cited here applied to Christ, and is also applied in the second chapter of Revelation with reference to the Church. And yes, I know the sword is a metaphor referring to the preaching and declaration of God's gospel authority in this world. My only point here is that it is not a metaphor for bean bag or for group hugs. The Church *rules* in the name of Christ, and does so with a rod of *iron*. It does not rule by creating a cozy spot for everybody to hide in. The nations are smitten by it. And when the nations are smitten, they then *submit*. And when a nation submits to the authority of Christ, what do you have? You have a Christian nation.

It is important to note here that I am talking about spiritual authority through the gospel. The Church is not supposed to be wielding any temporal swords at all.

But Boyd doesn't want this metaphorical sword to have any potency whatever. He wants the nations to be smitten, and he wants the result of this to be that they take no notice whatever. Read through this string of quotes.

> Which is to say, nothing is more important than that we keep the kingdom of God distinct from the kingdom of the world, both in our thought and in our actions.[66]

---

66  Ibid., 53–54.

By definition, therefore, you can no more have a Christian
worldly government than you can have a Christian petu-
nia or aardvark.[67]

The all-important distinction between the kingdom of
God and the kingdom of the world entails that a king-
dom-of-God citizen must take care never to align any
particular version of the kingdom of the world with the
kingdom of God. We may firmly believe one version to
be better than another, but we must not conclude that
this better version is therefore closer to the kingdom of
God than the worse version.[68]

In the second Psalm, the rod of iron wielded by Christ and
His people (again a *spiritual* authority) smashes the pottery of
nations to bits. When it comes to actual physical and civic authority, this is wielded by the civil authority—which is Christian,
but not ecclesiastical. But in Boyd's world, the pots don't ever
find out that they have been shattered. They continue on, just as
powerful as ever. Boyd wants to keep the kingdom of God separate from the kingdom of the world, because if they come into
contact, there might be a battle, and if there were to be a battle,
who knows? *We might win it.* And because we can't have *that*,
we withdraw. In Boyd's scheme, we are to whack the nations for
their insolent ways, but we are to do it with Nerf rods.

Returning to the matter of discipleship and imitation,
when you first set yourself to imitating Jesus seriously, you
have to *look* at Him. And when you look at Him carefully, you

67   Ibid., 54.
68   Ibid.

see more than a Yoder usually can see. You not only see Him forgiving prostitutes, you also see Him *praise centurions*. But Boyd can't see this—once again he leaves out the centurions. "Once we understand that the kingdom looks like Jesus, attracting tax collectors and prostitutes, serving the sick, the poor, and the oppressed, it is as obvious when it is present as it is when it is absent."[69] But Boyd is just using words for effect here without thinking about what he is actually saying. For Jesus to associate with the tax collectors was not an association with the oppressed. It was an association with the despised, all right, but with despised *oppressors*. The tax collectors were the guys who could send a SWAT team to your house, for Pete's sake. The people who despised the tax collectors were actually the ones taking the side of the oppressed. The prostitutes really were a rejected and oppressed class, and Jesus associated with them, also. And then, busting all of Boyd's paradigms, Jesus would also go have dinner with centurions at the Officer's Club. He would eat with prostitutes *and* with Pharisees. *And* with a captain in the Marine Corps.

There was one odd concession that Boyd makes, but I cannot figure out how he can fit it into his larger scheme of things. "To be sure, a version of the kingdom of the world that effectively carries out law, order, and justice is indeed closer to God's will for *the kingdom of the world*. Decent, moral people should certainly encourage this as much as possible, whatever their religious faith might be."[70]

---

69  Ibid., 53.
70  Ibid., 55.

This is good, so far as it goes, because it means that Boyd is rejecting the absurd doctrine of moral equivalence—a doctrine which would equate the ravaging genocides of Stalin with topless sunbathing in France. But what on earth could he mean—God's will for the kingdom of the world? Is it really God's will that nations continue to disbelieve in His Son (note Boyd's phrase here, "whatever their religious faith might be")? Is it comparatively God's will for nations to be secular states? Is God mandating that our laws be based on something other than His revealed will? And so if we institute the Ten Commandments into our law, we are *disobeying* Him? And if we implement "law, order, and justice" defined in a secular way without reference to Him, we are obeying Him *kind of*? This is deep theology and it's no wonder I'm lost.

Many of our prophetic voice brethren are willing, like Jonah, to speak truth to power. They, also like Jonah, would be entirely flummoxed if power listened to them.

Jonah's reluctance to preach to Nineveh was not driven by cowardice or anything like that. He hated Nineveh, a godless power, an oppressor of Jonah's people, and he knew that if he preached to them, there was a very real risk that they might repent and that God might accept their repentance. And repent they did (Mt. 12:41), and Jonah's complaint was one he anticipated. Isn't this disaster what I *said* would happen (Jon. 4:2)? If there is one thing worse than a godless power structure in Nineveh, that would be a Constantinian power structure in Nineveh. Hear what I'm sayin'?

And so here is the trick. If your whole schtick is that of being a prophetic voice, then you have to figure out what to do about the off-chance of real repentance. If *that* happened, then not only would the inhabitants of Nineveh repent in dust and ashes, but your whole political theology would have to repent in dust and ashes, also, and that would be a bummer. Whatever happens, we have to keep your radical political theology. If we want to keep your theology cutting edge, we have to make sure it never cuts anything.

And so it is necessary for the Anabaptists to configure the preaching in such a way that repentance is structurally impossible. Define Constantinianism as a heresy and figure out ways to identify the presence of that heresy regardless of what happens. Find it in coercion and find it in the soft coercion of no coercion. Find it in established churches and find it nations where the churches are not established, but are influential. Find it where the churches are marginalized and not influential at all. Meet the challenge! Find it when the magistrate goes right, when he goes left, and when he stays put. Whatever you do, find that heresy, and you can soothe your ruffled Jonah feathers with this: Nineveh didn't *really* repent.

The attendance of Constantine at the Council of Nicea was striking, but more striking than that was the existence of such a subversive council in the first place, and with an emperor's knowledge and blessing. It is often said that, in his conversion, Constantine was only seeking a unifying principle for his sprawling empire, and that his faith in Christ was not sincere. In some respects, whether or not his faith was sincere is beside the point, although I do think it was genuine. But what makes us think that the two motives are inconsistent? A man might come to Christ because he wants to save his marriage, but this does not make him a hypocrite.

Another commonplace with regard to Constantine is that he was freaked out by the Arian controversy because it threatened to undo his *realpolitik* principle of unity right after he had adopted it. Right after he bet the imperial farm on the Christian horse, that horse got the staggers.

But why would Constantine have seen the Church as a principle of unity in the first place? The unity displayed by the Church, in the simple fact of such councils, was something that the ancient Church had not really seen before. It was a new thing in the world. Rome had its Senate, but that was local, for the Romans. The Romans in turn ruled the world, but they did so in true top-down fashion. The traffic flow of authority went outward from Rome. In the Church councils, you see the development of a recognizable, universal representative form of decision-making. It dealt with the things of God, true enough, but this was a senate gathered from over a huge geographical area.

So the Christians were not supplying something that the pagan religions had previously supplied back before their sacrificial fires became impotent. The Christians brought something new. That idea was a visible demonstration of what true representative unity might look like. There is something enormously attractive to everyone in this. We see a secularist (and grotesque) parody of the idea in the United Nations. Whenever worldlings try to produce the fruit of faith on their own, without Jesus, the result is that Iran gets a seat on the body safeguarding women's rights, and the Chicoms get to weigh in on the importance of human rights. The result, in short, is a sort of globo-joke. In other words, without Jesus, *fuhgedaboudit*.

The fact remains that the thing that Constantine saw was altogether lovely. "My righteousness is near; my salvation is gone forth, and mine arms shall judge the people; the isles shall wait upon me, and on mine arm shall they trust" (Is. 51:5). But, in fact, it was the kind of loveliness that cannot be sustained for more than five minutes without Jesus Christ.

What Constantine saw was just a glimpse, a foretaste. It was a cloud the size of a man's fist. The prophet's words are being fulfilled, but they are not entirely fulfilled yet. We still await the latter rains–which *are* coming.

So I have made a great deal out of the Great Commission, where Jesus tells His apostles to disciple the nations. I have noted that the direct object of that verb is the *ethne*, plural of *ethnos*—the people, the tribe, the whole unit.

This means the question has arisen whether I am overlooking the explanatory participles following—baptizing and teaching. Since we don't literally immerse a nation, or pour water on it, doesn't this mean that the common reading, that of fetching disciples out of all the nations, is permissible? No, but if this were a one-off passage on the subject, it certainly would be a reasonable take. Here is why I am not persuaded.

First, I accept the fact that preaching to, baptizing, and teaching individuals is foundational. No getting away from it, no getting around it. But it is basic to the New Testament approach to this that there are no excepted individuals. We are told to preach the gospel to *every* creature (Mk. 16:15). We are told that the gospel ignores basic social distinctions of rank (Gal. 3:28). The early converts did not contain a large majority of the world's nobility (1 Cor. 1:26), but it did contain a goodly number of them (Acts 13:1, 12). In other words, the gospel is to be preached *to all men without distinction.* We are to pray for kings and all those in authority (1 Tim. 2:2), and among other reasons this is because God wants all *kinds* of men to be saved and come to a knowledge of the truth (1 Tim. 2:4). When a high official with Queen Candace's court was riding along with Philip, they were talking about the great sacrifice of the Suffering Servant in Isaiah 53. Suddenly, the eunuch requests baptism. Why would he do that? Just one verse before the passage they were discussing, we find this: "So shall he sprinkle *many nations*; the *kings* shall shut their mouths at him: for that which had not been told them shall they see; and that which they had not heard shall they consider" (Is. 52:15). Now I don't want to start the blood-hounds of baptismal mode baying off in another direction. It is enough for me here that the *kings* shut their mouths. And this is why we see the evangelistic instinct in Paul come right to the surface when he is talking to a king (Acts. 26:28–29). In short, kings are included among the individuals that we must preach to.

Now, what happens when they listen? What happens when the king is converted and submits to baptism? What's next in the Commission? We teach him obedience to every word that proceeds from the mouth of God. We teach obedience to all things that Christ commanded. When we lead a stable hand to Christ, we baptize him and then teach him obedience. Among other things, we teach him not to lean on his shovel so much (Eph. 6:6). If he is a magistrate, his lessons after baptism should include how to establish his throne in righteousness (Prov. 16:12), how to banish scamps and rascals from the court (Prov. 25:5), and how to stop debasing the currency (Is. 1:22). So my first point is that kings are people, too.

The second argument for this concerns the foundation for Christ's claim of authority in the Great Commission. He doesn't tell his disciples to go, He tells them *therefore to* go. That *therefore* is critical, because it links our mission to the universal authority of Christ over every other authority that can be named, which obviously includes the authorities in the nations you are preaching to. Now Jesus was not just winging it when He said this. He was fulfilling all that the prophets had spoken in everything that He said and did. There are many places in the Old Testament that confirm this, but let me pick one of the more obvious—when it comes to the subject of kings. Remember we are talking about sin, death, resurrection, authority, and conversion—with regard to kings.

Let's walk through it, and I will keep my comments brief.

"Why do the heathen rage, and the people imagine a vain thing? The kings of the earth set themselves, and the rulers take counsel together, against the Lord, and against his anointed, saying, Let us break their bands asunder, and cast away their cords from us" (Ps. 2:1–3). This passage is quoted in Acts 4:25–28 and is applied to the crucifixion of Jesus. So we know we are talking about the death of the Messiah, and this also helps define what sort of authorities we are talking about in this Psalm.

"He that sitteth in the heavens shall laugh: the Lord shall have them in derision. Then shall he speak unto them in his wrath, and vex them in his sore displeasure. Yet have I set my king upon my holy hill of Zion" (Ps. 2:4–6). God laughs at them, and the reason is that He has established *His* king in Zion, and so their plans will all come to nothing.

"I will declare the decree: the Lord hath said unto me, Thou art my Son; this day have I begotten thee" (Ps. 2:7). So this is the decree. God declares that Jesus is His Son. Anticipated in the baptism of Jesus, He does this ultimately in the resurrection (Rom. 1:4). God has also shown in the resurrection that Jesus will judge the nations (Acts 17:31). And clinching this point, Paul says that this verse is a prophecy of the resurrection (Acts 13:33).

Now, what happens in Psalm 2, right after the resurrection? *"Ask of me, and I shall give thee the heathen for thine inheritance, and the uttermost parts of the earth for thy possession"* (Ps. 2:8). What happens is that Jesus is given *all authority*—the authority He wielded when He told His apostles to go and disciple the nations, baptizing them and teaching them to obey everything He said.

"Thou shalt break them with a rod of iron; thou shalt dash them in pieces like a potter's vessel" (Ps. 2:9). Never forget that the New Testament teaches us what the Old Testament means. This verse is quoted three times in the book of Revelation. Twice it is applied to the complete authority of Jesus over the nations (Rev. 12:5; 19:15). In the other place, it refers to the fact of our shared authority with Him over the nations (Rev. 2:27). And why? Because we are kings and priests on the earth (Rev. 5:10).

And so what is the conclusion of this matter? "Be wise now therefore, *O ye kings*: be instructed, ye judges of the earth. Serve the Lord with fear, and rejoice with trembling. Kiss the Son, lest he be angry, and ye perish from the way, when his wrath is kindled but a little. Blessed are all they that put their trust in him" (Ps. 2:10–12). Because Jesus died and rose, and because He has all authority now, the kings of the earth (the same kind that crucified Him) are commanded to be wise, to be instructed, to serve Him with fear, to rejoice with trembling, and to kiss the Son. They are commanded to put their trust in Him. In short, the kings of the earth *are to receive Christian baptism*, and they are to bring their honor and glory into the Christian Church (Rev. 21:24–26).

To the extent that the kings of the earth are separated from the people of God, to that same extent they are being disobedient. These are not two separated kingdoms. These are spheres that can be distinguished, but they have their point of unity in the one true King over all, even Jesus. If there are two *distinct* houses among men, they are the house of healing (and the leaves from the tree of life are for the healing of the nations), and the house of sin and pestilence.

What do we do in the gospel proclamation? We summon all the people, and we do not exclude the king. We approach the king, shut up like Uzziah in his lazar house, and invite him to come out, to come worship in the sanctuary. A true poultice from the leaves of healing and life has already been prepared.

For the sake of argument, let me grant all the atrocities that were perpetrated by this "Christian nation" of ours. Line them all up: *in accordance with the argument of this book*, what would Boyd have had us do if we had been there watching the floggings, the massacres, the kidnappings, the slaving, the rapes, the thefts, the treaty-breaking? What would Boyd's version of love have had us *do*? The answer—his way of fine-talking humility and surpassing love—is *nothing*.

"Jesus—who, incidentally, never allowed himself to get pulled into the political disputes of his day."[71]

Are women getting raped? Don't get pulled in. Are children being hauled off to work in factories? Don't get pulled in. Are treaties being flagrantly broken? That's just the way the world is, ya know? Are thousands of slaves being pitched overboard into the Atlantic? Satan's kingdom . . . what can you do? Spiritually dangerous even to try.

Whenever the question of violence arises, Boyd will describe only ungodly violence poured out over the heads of innocent victims. And he is guilty of two terrible things here. First, he never describes a warrior, a Christian knight,

---

71  Ibid., 11.

stepping in between a victim and a malicious attacker. It is as though Boyd doesn't believe this can ever happen. But I can assure you that *he* lives in a very comfortable world precisely because it does happen.

I can condemn wicked violence, and I do. I can condemn, heartily, every atrocity that Boyd wants to dig up. "Slaughtering, enslaving, cheating, conquering, and dominating are not the sort of activities Jesus engaged in!"[72] Right. Fine. Amen. Give me something difficult to affirm. But Boyd is incapable of praising godly violence, and this is because he is living in the dream castle of Christianity, which is so far up in the clouds that it does not even need a security system. But for the rest of us, "Blessed *be* the Lord my strength, which teacheth my hands to war, *and* my fingers to fight" (Ps. 144:1).

But far worse than the first problem, Boyd describes these horrendous situations in such a way that *never* makes me wish that the Cherokee had had a couple thousand pacifists standing on the sidelines wringing their hands. And after carrying on this way, he has the bronzed nerve to describe this principled *refusal* to take up the cause of the widow and orphan as *holiness*, as keeping the kingdom pure. Proceeding serenely from the undisputed dictum that we ought not use our armies to rape and murder widows and orphans, he acts like he has thereby proven that we must not use our armies to defend them.

72 Boyd, 100.

In the last chapter of the book, Boyd's pacifism comes out in full force, and he argues for it by answering the most common questions he receives whenever he addresses the themes of this book. Although many things could be said about all this, I want to limit myself to two.

First, the way Boyd approaches the imitation of Christ is highly inconsistent. "I think it is clear from Jesus' teachings, life, and especially his death that Jesus would choose nonviolence."[73] "Jesus didn't concern himself with fixing or steering the Roman government."[74]

Christ's example is of course authoritative for all Christians, but throughout this book, Boyd has mentioned that Jesus did *not* take an interest in politics. He was here to do something else. He did not get swept up into *our* issues. But suddenly this radical nonengagement becomes radical engagement via nonviolence, and that is a very different thing. Ghandi and Martin Luther King Jr. are mentioned glowingly in this chapter. Christians before the War Between the States should have (nonviolently) been involved in the Underground Railroad. But what happened to the imitation of Christ? Christ would heal a slave, for example, and that slave would stay a slave in the house of his centurion master (Mt. 8:13). What do we do with *that*? For Boyd, the imitation of Christ really is highly selective. Refusing to defend Himself. Check. Teaching us to overcome hate with love. Check. Making a whip to

73  Ibid., 166.
74  Ibid., 175.

clear the Temple. Ummm . . . Accepting centurions into His company. Uhhh . . .

To his credit, Boyd here does acknowledge the *existence* of a number of passages that seem to exclude his position (Lk. 3:14; Mt. 8:5–13; Lk. 7:1–10; Mk. 15:39; Acts 10:22, 34–35). He finally mentions the centurions, but, unlike prostitutes and tax-collectors, he keeps them at arm's length. "They also reveal that John the Baptist, Jesus, and earliest Christians gave military personnel 'space,' as it were, to work out the implications of their faith vis-à-vis their service."[75]

Whatever this is, it is not radical imitation, but rather selective imitation. Imitation of Christ becomes a nose of wax.

The second point concerns the nature of his dismissal of just war theory. It is at this point that the radical individualism of Boyd's position comes out (for all his talk of a *kingdom*). What is the problem with just war theory according to Boyd?

"Do you know—*can* you know—the myriad of personal, social, political, and historical factors that have led to any particular conflict and that bear upon whether or not it is justified . . . do you truly understand . . . are you certain . . . Are you certain . . . Are you certain . . . Do you know . . . Are you certain?"[76]

But of course just war theory is meant to be applied by those *making the decision* to go to war, and not to be applied by every infantryman or sailor who might be participating in the conflict. Those making the decision generally *do* have the facts they need to have in order to make a just decision,

75  Ibid., 168.
76  Ibid., 171.

and are accountable to God to do so. Those in the ranks do not have to weigh the ethics of every geopolitical event and, as Boyd points out, cannot do so. God doesn't require that of them. Individual Christians in the military must know what their duties are with regard to rejecting unjust and wicked behavior at *their* level of the conflict, and they must be prepared to refuse unlawful orders. But Boyd's criteria depend upon a democratic individualism that makes just war theory cumbersome and impossible.

This means that a Christian soldier may fight honorably in the eyes of God in a cause that is ultimately unjust. Moreover, a man might fight dishonorably in a just cause. Kings answer to God at their level, and soldiers at theirs. A Christian may not fight for a cause which he *knows* to be wicked, but if there is no manifest wickedness, he is not responsible to ascertain all the facts beforehand. He must be salt and light where he is, with the facts that he has.

# THE TWO KINGDOMS THAT WEREN'T

O f course I could not make much progress advocating "the Reformed Christian view of culture and politics" if I didn't mention a vocal demurring voice from within a wing of the Reformed Church itself. This is the Radical Two-Kingdom option, or R2K for short. This view has come close to the Anabaptist view, all the while claiming to be the historical Reformed position of the two kingdoms. Representatives of this view would include Michael Horton, D.G. Hart, and David VanDrunen. Another representative of this would be Jason Stellman, who argued for this position in his book *Dual Citizens*. Michael Horton wrote the foreword, and the sentiment there can be summed up as "This world is not my home; I'm just passing through." The Christian life is a pilgrimage (which Horton aptly distinguishes from tourism), and he notes (also aptly) how the Word and sacrament, publicly ministered, "provide the right coordinates for our pilgrimage," for we have a precarious location at the intersection of this present evil age and the age to come.[77] This whole book is structured around the theme of "already and not yet." And of course every orthodox Christian holds to this, but there are still some important questions that we have to hang from this particular formulation. *What* is already? *What* is not yet?

In addressing this matter of two kingdoms, I have previously mentioned that we could be fine with that term, but we should insist on knowing how many kings there are. Not every two-kingdom theology is the two-kingdom theology of the Reformers. The answer for Christians (of course) has to be that Christ is the king of all—but in contemporary two-kingdoms thought there is a tendency to grant this, but then to take away with the left hand what was given with the right. For example, Stellman concludes his dedication by thanking his congregation, which faithfully listens to him preach and teach, "week in and week out, in one form or another, about the difference between the earthly kingdom *of man* and the heavenly kingdom of Christ" (emphasis mine).[78] If there is only one king, shouldn't this have been the earthly kingdom of Christ and the heavenly kingdom of Christ?

77  Jason Stellman, *Dual Citizens: Worship and Life Between the Already and the Not Yet* (Orlando, FL: Reformation Trust Publishers, 2009), xi. It should be noted somewhere that since writing this book, Stellman has departed from the Reformed faith for Rome.

78  Ibid.

We can acknowledge this much agreement at least. Stellman says that eschatology "precedes *everything*."[79] Amen. Eschatology bears "directly on so many aspects of the Christian life."[80] Amen again—it bears on everything. And because it bears on everything, we need to be clear about everything.

But being clear about everything means that we should not allow ourselves to fall into false dilemmas.

"Do we American Christians obey the fourth commandment by worshiping on the Lord's Day primarily to recapture the former glory of the United States, or do we withdraw from cultural activity on Sunday in order to demonstrate to the culture that, on this day at least, our heavenly citizenship eclipses our identities as citizens of the civil kingdom of man."[81] That's it? Those are our choices? Sabbath keeping to recover American glory or Sabbath keeping to carve out at least *one* day for God, while leaving six to man? My choices are limited to whether America gets six days of my time or seven? Note also the juxtaposition (again) of heavenly citizenship under Christ and civil citizenship under *man*. Contrary to all this, it seems to me that our heavenly citizenship should eclipse our earthly citizenship *all the time*. I am not an American for six days and a Christian for one. Rather, I am a baptized Christian all the time, a husband all the time, a father all the time, a neighbor all the time, and a citizen all the time. And I have to figure out the hierarchical layers of these

79  Ibid., xiii. Emphasis his.
80  Ibid.
81  Ibid., xiv.

responsibilities, according to Scripture, and, you guessed it, I
have to do this all the time.

"Our dual citizenship, then, allows us to wait eagerly for
eternal glory while seeing the temporal blessings of earth
as gifts of God not to be feared but enjoyed."[82] But this is
a misstatement of the problem, offered in quite a dramatic
way. The problem is not the *not yet* of heavenly bliss and the
*already* of beer. We are not comparing pleasure to pleasure,
but rather ultimate responsibilities to *temporal responsibilities*. If it were just a matter of temporal pleasure, Stellman
and I could come to an agreement quickly. We could both
say grace over the beer, the mashed potatoes, the gifts of
marriage, and so on. We could both receive all these blessings in the name of Jesus, and amen. But could we both
fight Nazis in the name of Jesus? Could we contend for the
unborn in the name of Jesus? Could we insist on honest
weights and measures in the marketplace in the name of
Jesus? If so, there goes the debate. If not, then why not? If
Jesus is the King over this world, then why this strange superstition about naming Him?

"The central thesis of this book is that the new covenant
situates us in a tension between 'the already' on the one hand
and the 'not yet' on the other."[83] Like I said, we all agree with
this, and we will continue to agree until someone suggests
some concrete details for what is to be settled "already," before
the eschaton. The tension ought not to be between getting to

82  Ibid., xv.
83  Ibid., xiii.

confess the name of the Lord in the eschaton, and not getting to confess Him now. That is not the tension. The tension,
rather, ought to be that of confessing Him faithfully now in
the face of stiff opposition and being welcomed by Him at
the last day as one who did so. We are *pilgrims*, not Trappist
monks. We get to *say* where we are going and why. We are
privileged to relate every aspect of our behavior on the way to
the fact that we are being pilgrims. We are not called to tiptoe
and mime our way across the public square.

"God has only one 'nation,' and that is the church."[84] Obviously, I would modify this somewhat. God has only one *royal*
priesthood, only one *holy* nation, and that is the Church (1
Pet. 2:9). And because of the glory radiating from this beautiful city, the kings of the earth bring their honor and glory into
it. In this wonderful city, on the trees that grow on both sides
of the river, what kind of leaves are grown? The kind that heal
the nations (Rev. 22:2). How many nations does God have in
this sense? *All* of them.

So Stellman does a good job nailing those who have jum-
bled up their Christian faith with their heartland, red-state
patriotism. When that particular jumble gets knocked, we
should just let matters unfold. The United States does not
carry "redemptive significance."[85] Amen.

But there is still a difference in the background, not surprisingly. The United States *does* carry redemptive significance in
one sense—in the sense that sinners in need of redemption

84  Ibid., xv.
85  Ibid.

carry redemptive significance. We are a sinful nation, like all the nations. We therefore need salvation. But needing salvation (a salvation which is promised to us, incidentally) is a far cry from being a savior.

Surprisingly, however, Stellman does rebuke the outside world in a fashion that I had not believed consistent with the stance he is urging. "In fact, our collective blind spots often keep us from recognizing in ourselves the same faults that we criticize in other cultures (Jesus spoke about this, saying that it is somewhat disingenuous to lament the speck in another's eye while ignoring the plank in one's own, Matt. 7:1–6)."[86] What do the words of Jesus have to do with cultures outside the Church? When Jesus said not to do that, wasn't He talking to His baptized disciples *within* the Church?

> We can wonder with great sanctimony how antebellum Southerners could claim to be disciples of Jesus while being owners of slaves, but when a Fortune 500 company moves its manufacturing operations to sweatshops in Malaysia so it can pay the workers $.09 an hour without having to worry about labor laws to protect them from oppression, we don't call that 'slave-owning,' we call it 'smart business.' We watch World War II documentaries and wonder how the German population could sit back passively as Jews were slaughtered by the train-full, while feeling no guilt over the tens of thousands of innocent men, women, and children who have been killed while we liberate Iraq. Though the world and its lusts may take a different form in our

86  Ibid., 71.

country than in those 'heathen lands afar,' they are still alive, well, and largely characteristic even of a free and democratic society such as our own.[87]

This is prophetic indignation on the cheap. If you don't have anything to say to the nations, then don't say it. If you don't have anything to say to the nations, don't spend time telling us what you *would* say, had you only gotten around to it. And if you do have something to say, then tell them how their sins displease God, and tell them to repent and believe. Tell them to kiss the Son lest He be angry. But that is verging on the edge of a transformational impulse.

Cash this out. Stellman has said a number of things in the quote above about the other kingdom that amount to a stinging rebuke. But is it really a stinging rebuke? Every one of those things is the kind of thing that Christian pastors have to deal with, because their members live out six days of every week in that other kingdom. And life in that other kingdom brings more obligations with it than the obligation to put your trash out by the curb on the right day. In that other kingdom, Christians are board members of said Fortune 500 companies, and they vote on whether to move the factory or not. They are in the reserves and they get called up to go to Iraq. What do they *do*? One thing they should not have to put up with is their pastors rebuking them for being good "German Christians" while at the same time telling them to go right ahead.

87  Ibid., 71.

Stellman said earlier in the book that believers are to undertake these tasks in a different way, but in the dilemmas
outlined above, a different way would entail a different *direction*. We are talking about more than putting the trash by
the curb with a cheerful disposition as opposed to a grumpy
one. Now, does Jesus have opinions about such *directions*? If
He does, the Christians involved should do what they can
to make it go that direction—which is transformational and
against Stellman's whole project. But if Jesus has no opinion
about it, then His pastors shouldn't preach about it or write
about it.

We can't have it both ways. We can't halt between two opinions.

Stellman asserts that this world's activities are ultimately
pointless because they exist in time. "In a word, *time renders
all of man's earthly pursuits utterly pointless*."[88] He appears to
be making this point about the passage of created time itself,
and not the passage of fallen time or fallen history "under
the sun." This appears to me to be very dangerous. It locates
pointlessness and futility, not in sin and rebellion where it
belongs, but rather in something that God created and pro-
nounced good before there was any sin or rebellion.

"And the earth brought forth grass, and herb yielding
seed after his kind, and the tree yielding fruit, whose seed
was in itself, after his kind: *and God saw that it was good.*
And the evening and the morning *were the third day*" (Gen.
1:12–13). God created time, and it was good. It was not
subject to futility.

---

88  Ibid., 104. Emphasis his.

This creates trouble and difficulty at the other end of history, as well. We will be raised from the dead as human beings, and we will live forever as glorified men and women. If the glorification of humanity entails the removal of time, it is difficult to see in what way we can look forward to it. The discontinuity between this life and the next is no longer the discontinuity between dishonor and honor or between corruption and lack of corruption, but rather a discontinuity between life in heaven and on earth and life in the seventeenth dimension. In short, this equation of futility with the mere existence of time appears to confound a creational good with sin. But man fell into sin. He didn't fall into time.

A second problem lies with Stellman's handling of the natural revelation of Romans 1. "This god, Paul explained, does not save anyone, for the book of nature reveals a naked god of law, of justice, and of seeming indifference to human pain . . . . Nature's god appears as an absentee landlord, an insignificant other who may be *there*, but who is certainly not *here* . . . . And even if he is out there, he appears to be too indifferent to listen, too holy to help, too transcendent to touch, and too vengeful to invoke."[89]

This is honestly hard to fathom. Stellman is treating the God of Romans 1 as though He were an inscrutable power, distant and far removed. But Paul says precisely the opposite. The problem is not sinners wishing they could somehow attain to knowledge of God. They *have* knowledge of God, and it sticks to them in a way they hate. They cannot turn around

89  Ibid., 108.

without seeing the God who reveals Himself plainly in every leaf on every tree, and they take this truth, and they *suppress* it in flagrant unrighteousness. What Stellman makes distant, Paul brings near. Paul uses words like *manifest, revealed, clearly seen*, and *understood*. In Paul's assessment, there is no distance between God and man, but also no fellowship. Again, the problem is *sin*, not distance.

The way Stellman describes the problem, we feel sorry for the sinners who have to deal with a *Deus absconditus*. The way Paul describes it, we see the righteousness of God's wrath visited upon those who insisted on having nothing to do with the God in whom they lived and moved and had their being.

I am not sure why Stellman would make this kind of move, unless it is to keep the realm outside the Church (which is where natural revelation preaches) free of all explicit obligations to Jesus Christ. But Paul preached the true name of the unknown God to the Athenians. And here in Romans, he was not preaching the name of the known God into obscurity. The God who *reveals* Himself to all men is the true God, the Father of the Lord Jesus Christ, and the one who sent the Holy Spirit into the world. The God of Romans 1 is *not* a generic god, and He is not inscrutable. The miserable wretches described in Romans 1 only *wish* He were inscrutable.

That said, on to a critical point. Stellman sets before us two of God's saints who left Egypt in different ways—Joseph and Moses. Joseph came a slave and died a prince. Moses grew up as a prince and left with all the slaves. Joseph left after he died, when his bones were moved. Moses left before he died.

But both of them clearly held the riches of Egypt at just the right level of esteem.

And here is where I have to commend Stellman for seeing and acknowledging something that is frequently not seen in these discussions. It is at least a good beginning. He quotes the entirety of Hebrews 11:33–38, and notes how the writer

> moves seamlessly from those whose faith resulted in their conquering kingdoms and stopping the mouths of lions to those whose faith resulted in their being imprisoned or sawn in two. The point of presenting so stark a contrast with such a cavalier nonchalance is stated near the end of this section—neither the triumphs associated with the victorious saints of verses 33–35 nor the defeats of those described in verses 36–38 are 'worthy' of drawing their subjects' attention away from the enduring blessing of 'receiving a kingdom that cannot be shaken' (12:28).[90]

Amen. This is super important. This is hyper important. This is good old regular important.

But what I don't understand is why the positive side of this kind of achievement "by *faith*" is off the table in the new covenant. Yes, there are thundering dominionists who know not what spirit they are of. When you try to do anything right, this is the kind of world where it is easy to veer off into wrong. This applies to all kinds of Christian political action. But men go to the stake in this fallen world, and martyrdom is no infallible protection against the subtleties arrayed against us. If

90 Ibid., 110.

I give my body to be burned, and have not love, I am *nothing*. But how could this be worked into an argument about the dangers of giving up everything for Jesus Christ? How could it be turned into an argument on the follies of martyrdom?

When you enroll in a math class, *you will have math problems*. Those math problems are not an argument for staying out of the class. When you resolve to follow Jesus Christ, you will have "following Jesus Christ" problems. If He gives you victory, you will have victory temptations, like Gideon. If He gives you the opportunity to doubt Him while in prison awaiting execution, like John the Baptist, you will have *those* kinds of problems.

We can fail at being well-fed. We can fail at being hungry. Or we can learn from the apostle Paul in both conditions. It is not the case that temptations await us if we seek to engage in the culture wars, but not if we disengage. And the possibility of spiritual failure in both directions is not an argument for not taking up the cross that the Lord assigns to us. God wants some men to be Jeremiah and others to be Moses. He wants some to be King Alfred and others Bonhoeffer. Some godly men head up armies that lose and others head up armies that win. *Both* are called to do what they do in the world in the name of Jesus Christ, and with true evangelical *faith*. The kingdom of God is not a "one size fits all" operation. This is not affected by whether the kingdom of God as a whole enjoys temporal and historical success in this world.

The bottom line is this: there is absolutely no inconsistency between wanting the nations to acknowledge Jesus Christ

THE TWO KINGDOMS THAT WEREN'T 

and laboring for their conversion, on the one hand, and acknowledging that nothing will finally and ultimately be put right until the resurrection, even if the nations are fully converted, as I believe they will be.

So the question is, can the kind of successes enjoyed in Hebrews 11 be imitated by new covenant saints? Are these things we may do in the name of Jesus?

Another "problem" like this appears in Darryl Hart's book, *A Secular Faith*. He begins by noting that many American conservative Christians take comfort in the idea of a president praying for strength and guidance —"at best innocent if not becoming."[91] Isn't it good for the most powerful man in the world to "acknowledge his dependence upon powers mightier than his rather than proudly thinking he could manage on his own?"[92] The pleasant thought experiment goes down quite well.

"But complications ensued when the group of conservatives considered the hypothetical of someone like Hillary Rodham Clinton offering a prayer for help in her conduct as chief executive of the United States. At this point the image turned from consoling to annoying, even alarming."[93]

You bet it does. But Hart thinks that this exposes "the inconsistency that so often accompanies the way Americans mix Christianity and politics. Just the thought of Clinton beseeching divine favor drives conservatives crazy, the thought

91  Darryl Hart, *A Secular Faith: Why Christianity Favors the Separation of Church and State* (Chicago, IL: Ivan R. Dee, 2006), ix.
92  Ibid., ix.
93  Ibid., x.

of Bush doing so is equally infuriating to liberals and Democrats."[94] But this should lead to the next question—who is right to react this way? Or are they both wrong? To react from the mere *fact* of different reactions into agnosticism about God's will for the political realm is way more conclusion than these premises will bear.

"The point of this book is to try to complicate contemporary understandings of the relationship between Christianity and liberal democracy in the United States . . . . It starts from the premise that Christianity is an apolitical faith."[95]

Now that is quite a premise. And if that is the premise, we should not be surprised if the conclusion looks quite a bit like it. The sons of Abraham do the works of Abraham. But why should we start with an axiomatic assumption that the Christian faith, which has had more of a political impact than any other force in the world, is apolitical?

"Historically the Christian religion, with the major exception of its American expression, has been concerned not with life, liberty, and the pursuit of happiness, but with salvation from sin and death."[96]

Okay, this should be lively. Before we get to our substantive disagreement, there is a point here that I find to be simply odd. Hart is saying that the historic Christian faith has not been so much concerned with politics as it has been with saving our souls. The American Christians, in this view, are

94  Ibid.
95  Ibid.
96  Ibid.

all about life, liberty, and the pursuit of happiness. But this construct seems to me almost a photo negative of the truth. When Constantine convened the Council of Nicea, was he assiduously avoiding undue Church–state entanglements? When Phillip II corresponded with Pope Sixtus about funding the Armada against Elizabethan England, what was that? Getting souls into heaven apart from politics has been the unique American truncation. The most ardent evangelical lobbyist in D.C. is *nothing* compared to the millennium and a half of established churches, a practice which American Christians successfully rejected for the first time in the history of Christendom. As I say, that point is just a bit odd.

But here is the substantive issue. The message of Christ *is* about deliverance from sin and death. But do sin and death remain internally located in each individual soul, or do sin and death ever come *out?* Do they have any cultural forms and expressions? Do sin and death ever shape the *polis?* When a people sin in three dimensions, and they demand that the throne be established on unrighteousness, and they frame iniquity with a law, and they say that a woman can have her child dismembered in the womb as her constitutional right, does the Church, with its message of deliverance from sin and death, have anything to say about all this sin and death?

And when a professing Christian leader fights tenaciously for the right of women to chop babies into pieces, and is someday elected to the presidency while running on that platform, would Christians be right to be outraged at her professions of Oval Office piety? Sure. They would be wrong not to do so, because faith without works is dead. I would be distressed at President Hillary's claims to have sought the divine guidance for the same reasons I would be just as distressed if she were the Anglican Archbishop of Somewhere-or-Other, making the same claims and disregarding the Bible just as blithely. We can hold her professions of piety *up against what the Bible says*. If we can't do that, then why have Bibles at all?

Incidentally, I am making this argument so that Christians may call their leaders to righteousness, whether those leaders are Republicans or Democrats. I am not assuming that only Democrats are guilty of this kind of hypocrisy—far from it. When these words were first written, the present writer was being represented in the United States Senate by Larry Craig, the Terror of Minneapolis.

When Herod stole his brother's wife, the approach of John the Baptist was a tad simplistic. He just went up there and said that it is not lawful to do that. Should Herod have replied that John needed to get back to his parish to work on his sermon? "Don't meddle in politics, John. I've mentioned this before." John would have replied that he already *had* worked on his sermon, and he was delivering it *now*. "It is not lawful for you to have her."

Someone of Hart's intelligence and learning is incapable of writing a book without offering many penetrating insights, and this book is no exception. He starts out by observing the "tsunami of faith-based politics."[97] He objects to this, as he should, because government sponsorship of a generic faith,

---

97  Ibid., 3.

or groups that have "that faithy feel," is simply pragmatism. Christians should be no friends of any civic attempts to tear the "sectarian" heart out of the faith.

This is where someone like Hart is going to be at his strongest. The position he is critiquing *is* vulnerable, and vulnerable because flatly unscriptural. But the tendency will be for Hart to reject, for example, tax money going to support an ostensibly Christian soup kitchen because of the radical theocracy such an endeavor promises to promote, when actually the effort is thoroughly compromised and anemic. Such a case would not be an example of religion taking over the state; it would be the empire taking over a gaggle of deracinated religions. But there is a pro-Christendom argument that will not be vulnerable to this kind of critique at all. "But you want the government to become explicitly *Christian*." "Yes, you have understood our position exactly."

Hart says things that are just baffling. "But the present-day consensus about religion and American politics—that politics needs the ideals, inspiration, and morality of faith—is unprecedented."[98] What is *actually* unprecedented, in the history of the Church, is the novel idea that a culture can exist apart from a defining religious center, a *cultus*. After the War Between the States, America gradually inched into an experiment with this idea, and the Christians in this nation probably could have gone on with that idea indefinitely—but the secularists overplayed their hand, and began insisting on sodomite marriage and dismemberment of unborn children as prime examples of

98 Ibid., 5.

civic neutrality—"they are *personal* religious issues (*perhaps*), but certainly not areas where we have to listen to the voice of God." A lot of ordinary Christians saw this for what it was—a radical unveiling of the presence of an alien religion, one that *insists* on legislating in accordance with the will of *its* god.

But for all the surrounding confusion, Hart still frames the question perfectly. "What does Christianity require of its adherents politically? In applying this question to the relationship between faith and politics, rather than asking how much religion a liberal democracy can comfortably tolerate, the subject looks decidedly different."[99]

This is exactly right. To take liberal democracy as a given, and then to try to fit a faithy Christianity into it as a form of inspirational motivation, right alongside all the other faithy types of belief that are willing to cater to the secular overlords, is a fundamental compromise. Christians must not want their faith to be "befriended" by the powers that be, the only price being an abandonment of Christ and Him crucified.

But here is Hart's question again: what does Christianity require of its adherents politically? The answer is that, like Paul before Agrippa, we should desire our rulers to become just as we are, baptized and in submission to the Word of God. We should recognize that all authority in heaven and on earth has been given to Jesus, and that He used this as the basis for commanding us to disciple all the nations of men. We should want the establishment of a new and improved

99  Ibid., 11.

Christendom. We should tell the kings of the earth to kiss the Son, lest He be angry.

But Hart identifies himself as a "Christian secularist."[100] This creates a dilemma for him. Either he must walk away from the historic Reformed conviction about the lordship of Christ over all things (including politics), in which case *he* is the radical innovator, or he must say that Christian secularism is to be preferred because Jesus commands it, the Bible requires it, and so on. But this is way too stark. Imagine what texts you might appeal to in order to make the point that the kings and rulers of the earth should studiously avoid any reference to the true God, avoid listening to His Word in any kind of submission, and, above all, avoid rendering thanks to Him for His kindnesses. Imagine trying to prove from the Bible that God *wants* rulers, especially the Christian ones, to pretend that He doesn't exist—to pretend in public that they don't know Him.

Think of it another way. The United States could pass a constitutional amendment acknowledging the Lordship of Jesus Christ over all things, make Augustine the bishop of Des Moines, outlaw abortion and homosexual marriage, and Augustine could *still* have written his book *The City of God.* To say that the temporary governments of this world are *not* the Church of God is not the same thing as saying that they should not, or need not, be Christian. "Temporal" and "secular" *are not synonyms.* They used to be synonyms centuries ago, but no longer. The connotations have changed.

100  Ibid., 15.

If I owned a business, Wilson's Widgets, and I wanted that business to be Christian, which I would, being a Christian myself, I could do this without in any way believing that in the eschaton I was going to be presented with a brand-new Wilson's Widgets sign and a corner of glory land in which to set up shop. Just because something is not eternal does not give it the right to rebel against the authority of Jesus *now*, or to be agnostic about Him.

As we set about establishing the next Christendom, we must take care to avoid the pitfalls and grievous sins committed in the first one. But right now, we need to be avoiding another problem—our accommodation with the Enlightenment's take on secular neutrality, the idea that secularism is even *possible*. With that in mind, consider that John Colwell, summarizing Oliver O'Donovan, says that "secular authorities have been in serious trouble since Jesus rose from the dead; his rising marks their end both in the sense of their termination and in the sense of the revealing of the authentic goal and mediated authority; the most pressing danger for the Church is not that of illegitimately appropriating to itself such secular power *but rather of according to such secular power a legitimacy and significance that it no longer possesses*" (emphasis mine).

If I might, I would like to borrow a metaphor from Warfield and apply it to the phrase "the lordship of Christ." In the hands of liberals, the lordship of Christ is like pie dough—the farther you spread it, the thinner it gets. Hart shows how this has happened in the United States, tracing the origins of the phrase "one nation, under God" in the Gettysburg Address down to its insertion into the Pledge of Allegiance in 1954, when we were fending off the godless commies. And they *were* godless, and this did have ramifications, about which more later. I was born in 1953, so this means that I only lived in a heathen nation for one year.

Between the Gettysburg Address and the revised Pledge, a generic Protestantism tried hard to extend "the kingdom" over every aspect of life. But since this was a social gospel kind of thing, the kingdom was like pie dough. By the end of the process, we find ourselves saying that the lordship of Christ means that we have to put a brick in the back of the john to conserve water and that we have to drive a putt-putt car to save us all from global warming.

Of course, there is always the question of the facts. For example, if a public policy screecher began demanding that we all start rationing salt water because the planet Earth (which is our *only* home) was about to run completely out, and that many leading theologians agreed with this (and they *would*, too), and that they offered their agreement in the name of the Lord Jesus, and with many solemn *amens*, I would still want to know how they could possibly think we were going to run out of salt water.

There is also the question of what the lordship of Christ means, exactly. In my view, it means discipling the nations, baptizing them, and teaching them to obey everything Jesus commanded. It does not mean, just to be clear, invoking the name of Jesus in order to justify every damn fool idea that might be floating around in our heads. It means preaching the gospel in the narrow sense, saving souls, planting churches, building parish life, and then expecting the right worship of God in that place to transform that region over the course of centuries, and eventually to transform the world over the course of millennia. *Patience.*

I will grant to Hart the strong possibility that when Christians rush to implement kingdom ethics in the public square, they will frequently screw everything up. We need to make sure we are doing what Jesus said and not what we *thought* Jesus must have said. The textbook case against Christian activism can be made in one word—Prohibition—the word that would have made the Lord Jesus at Cana into a moonshiner felon. We did a great job there of setting aside the Word of God for the sake of our tradition. So we can fish around in Church history and find plenty of examples of Christians legislating against sin in ways that were ludicrous and embarrassing. And I, even though I want the authority of Jesus Christ recognized in the public square, will be suitably embarrassed. Not like *that*, I want to say. I am embarrassed by these things because they are done in the name of biblical law and at the same time are manifestly *unbiblical.*

A big part of the problem in sorting all this out arises when the state forgets its mission and place. Hart quotes a nineteenth-century Presbyterian named Robinson with approval, saying that "the state and the church had different ends. The state's was to restrain evil and cultivate social order; the church's was to save a remnant of the human race for the world to come."[101] So what do we do when the state refuses to re-strain evil, but rather perpetuates it on a massive scale, under-taking policies that are inimical to the social order? And I am not talking about the nickel-and-dime bureaucratic foul-ups either, but genocides, pogroms, abortion mills, and more. Does the Church continue on its very narrow mission of saving souls and, just like the priest and Levite in the Lord's story, refuse to look into the ditch by the side of the road? We sometimes miss a subtle twist in the parable. If these men stopped to help the guy and he turned out to be dead, this would render them ceremonially unclean, unfit to do the work of saving a remnant of the human race for the world to come.

Of course, if a secular state were keeping things contained in a halfway decent fashion, in an order-in-the-streets kind of way, Christians ought not to be agitating to get that thing "Christianized" tomorrow. We should be focusing on building worshiping communities—like Paul in the first part of Nero's reign. But as soon as the state catches on to what's happening in their midst (and they will), they will make sure to demand something that Christians cannot in good conscience render, and the conflict will be joined—as in the second half of Nero's reign. To illustrate, let me challenge Hart to a thought experi-ment. I will bestow on him one hundred worshiping churches, built to his exacting doctrinal specifications, with about two hundred faithful Christians in each one. We will plant those churches in Saudi Arabia, on the condition that Hart explain

101  Hart, 118.

to me how those churches could possibly be there without
causing a massive social, cultural, and political revolution.

I would be more than content to labor in the Church for a
cultural transformation that is still centuries out. The Church
is not in a hurry. I ask of the state only two things in return—
don't ask me for a pinch of incense for the emperor, and don't
undertake any civic enormities that would require a prophetic
denunciation from the Church. The conditions sound simple,
but this never happens, because part of the devil's strategy is
to make the Church confront these issues before the Church
is anywhere near ready to confront them. This is because you
always want to engage with your adversary *before* they get
their navy built.

Hart then brings up the very interesting idea of hyphenation.

"The idea of living a hyphenated existence—one part private and religious, the other part public and political—strikes
many as oxymoronic, and not just evangelical Protestants."[102]

Now I am afraid I am with the evangelical Protestants who
cannot make any sense out of this. And as I have shown elsewhere, this means that James Dobson is far more of a Westminsterian than Hart is on this issue, because James Dobson
is not a dualist like Hart is here.

I do cheerfully admit to all kinds of hyphenations in my
life, and every other Christian in the world deals with the
same kind of thing. But we have to understand the hyphenation correctly. There are many aspects of my identity that are
not essential to my standing in Christ. For example, I am a

102  Ibid., 174.

husband, an American, a conservative, a lover of the blues, a submariner, a son, and a minister. There are many fine Christians who are, to the contrary, wives, Englishmen, libertarians, jazz-lovers, aircraft carrier men, daughters, or laymen. This is why the hyphen must not set up a horizontal dualism, but rather point to a *hierarchy*. Whatever aspect of my identity exists in distinction from the legitimate identity of others must nevertheless be an aspect of my identity that is in submission to Christ. There is not one part of my life where Christ rules and another part where the "national character of public decisions" rule. I must go with the national character of the public decision *only if Jesus wants me to*.

The fact that Jesus wants all His children involved in a bunch of different pursuits is a Trinitarian thing and not an example of confusion. The hierarchies are ranked differently—they are not all the same. The Lord wants about half of his children to be husbands and the other half to be wives. He wants some to love classical music and others to love music from the Delta. He wants them all to hate abortion and child porn. He wants some to love the Palouse country of Idaho and others to love the pine forests of the South. And we should do what He calls us to do.

In the quote above, where Hart assumes that the religious part of me is private and the political part of me is public, it needs to be pointed it that it *does not follow* from the simple fact that we must live hyphenated lives. Yes, I am a husband, a conservative, a son, and so on. But the hierarchy simply means that I must be a Christian-husband, a Christian-conservative,

and a Christian-son. And whenever the demands of the two
come into conflict, I must always know which set of allegiances is required to give way.

Further, I have no more ground for saying that the religious is private and political is public than I have for saying
that my Christian life is private and devotional and that my
husbandly life is informed and shaped by *Cosmopolitan*, *Pent-
house*, and *Sex in the City*. And given the mere fact of the
dualistic hyphenation between private and public, why can't
I just switch what Hart has done here? Let's make the public
sphere Christian and the private life secular.

In short, simply the fact that different aspects of my identity can be described in different ways has nothing whatever to
do with whether Jesus is Lord over those different ways. The
only reason Hart can get away with all this is because a strict
isolation of Christian faith to the reservation of the heart is
something the Enlightenment has insisted upon, and it is a
surrender that those who have rejected the Westminsterian
tradition have made.

In other words, everything about me must be structured
according to the Word of God. My life in private is governed
by Scripture. My life in public is no different. It would be
most unfortunate if we came to the conclusion that Christ is
my Lord only when I am not being covered by the surveil-
lance cameras.

"Which invites the question: If it is possible to keep such
essential aspects of faith as prayer and almsgiving private,
even within the privacy of one's devotional life, why wouldn't

it be possible for a serious believer to keep that faith bracketed once entering the public square or the voting booth."[103]

"Keep that faith bracketed." Bracketed from *what*? What do you mean, *bracketed*? Let's take a simple case—a referendum is on your town's ballot on whether or not to give free condoms, sexual manuals, and KY lubricants to all eleven-year-olds. I am in the voting booth, and I have taken care to "bracket" my faith, whatever that is supposed to mean. How does that in any way *help* me? Does it mean the same thing as *suppress*?

I really think that this is an unfortunate reminder of what happens when you get in the grip of a bad idea. Jesus says not to let the right hand know what the left is doing—when you give alms, don't be a glory hound. But this is a secret—and not the same thing as private. The act of almsgiving is public and has public effects. When I am in the privacy of mailing an anonymous check to someone in need of it, how can that privacy be used as a model of voting for abortion funding in the privacy of the voting booth? In one secret chamber, I do good to someone, which is no license to do evil in another secret chamber. But if I refuse to do evil in the voting chamber (as I am confident that Hart refuses to do), then is this not an example of unsuccessful bracketing?

The state honors Jesus Christ by doing what Jesus Christ tells the state to do and not by doing whatever seemed like a great idea to somebody so long as the name of Jesus was invoked. If someone is celebrating a Kuyperian view of the

103  Ibid., 176.

Lordship of Christ over all things, I will rejoice with him. Yay. Go, dog, go. But I also want to reserve judgment just a little bit—because all kinds of cockamamie proposals have been advanced in the name of Jesus. Remember Prohibition. That particular public policy howler was instituted in the name of Jesus, but after that unfortunate Cana incident, it was a law that would have gotten Jesus hauled before the authorities three years earlier than He actually was. Not only did He manufacture about a hundred and sixty gallons of the stuff, He did so *without a license.*

Because statist agencies or state-controlled agencies are operating outside their assigned jurisdictional area, the necessary result is bungled compassion. At the end of the day, it is incompetent at best and cruel at worst. Christians should have nothing to do with any of it—because Jesus is Lord, and He told us to remember the poor. Compassionate conservatism is not compassionate because in the long run, it doesn't give a rip about the poor. The poor are the necessary fodder to make the public-private poverty industry run. Hope they stick around, and if they don't want to, we can help a little bit. As for conservativism, what is it conserving except for the budget appropriations that we managed to jam into the pork barrel last budget cycle?

My question is this, and it goes right to the inconsistent heart of the R2K theology. Can a minister of the gospel, in thus-saith-the-Lord mode, tell his parishioners and the broader Christian public that they have a moral obligation under Jesus Christ to live as businessmen, educators, citizens, masters, wives, husbands, or slaves in a particular way, as taught and informed by Scripture? I say *yes*. The R2K position says *no*.

Or rather, *wants* to say no, depending on the issue. Now that the shooting is done, and the issue of slavery is over a century old, R2K theology would like a piece of the action. The outside secular world disapproves of slavery *now*, and so it is safe for the Church to add her amen. But the world is not currently giving us the go-ahead for any opposition to public sodomy, for example.

The problem is that the Church cannot "leak" its moral standards on the issue of slavery only. When the Church is being the Church, we will have an impact on slavery, cocaine use, poverty, debt levels, abortions, and homosexual marriage. Salt with its savor affects everything. Salt without savor is trampled on by men, and Jesus says that such trampling is fitting. If we are going to have that effect, which Horton wistfully imagines for the nineteenth century, then why don't we go ahead and do it on purpose *now*? Can we deliberately seek to have this effect without being accused of purveying a Christless Christianity? Some of us are wishing that the Church would have the kind of impact on our *current* cultural atrocities that men like Horton wish for the Church of one hundred and fifty years ago.

The bottom line issue is this. If the Church is not transforming the culture around her, then the culture around her is transforming the Church. There is no static equilibrium point. That means that the Church will *either* be prophetically addressing the problem of gay mirage, or it will be in the process of adopting gay mirage herself. Either the Church will speak about the carnage of abortion and God's hatred of it, or the Church will be in the process of bringing that hated object into the sanctuary.

God did not send His Son into the world to form and establish the Church in order that this Church could float through the world like a ghost.

Behind the idea of Christendom is the matter of interpretive filters for your history. When it comes to evaluating whether things are getting better, staying the same, or getting worse, we will make that call in the grip of our foundational assumptions. Under the category of staying the same, we would also include a pattern of random ebb and flow.

For Christians, to have a genuinely Christian civil order develop would constitute an improvement. But do improvements actually happen? Everybody grants that particular improvements might happen—for example, my headache might go away—but, taking the long view, do overall improvements happen as history unfolds?

One of the things we must come to grips with is the fact that eschatology precedes everything. The last things come first, just like Jesus said. So the first thing we need to get hold of is the idea that the whole discussion is a matter of interpretative ideas in conflict, not an interpretive idea on one side and "the facts" on the other. Arthur Herman has done a wonderful job of showing that the idea of decline is in fact an *idea*, and so it is actually a school of thought—and not a bare mound of facts gathered from the newspapers.[104]

As an idea, it is capable of being refuted. As an idea, it should be possible for us to conclude that it is a bad idea. In our personal affairs, we all know the glass-half-empty people and the glass-half-full people. The former think of everything that could go wrong, and the latter think of all the positive possibilities. At some point in the proceedings, we should be able to demonstrate to some Gloomy Gus that it did not, in fact, rain on the picnic.

Progress is a biblical concept. Things have gotten better, they are better now, and they will continue to get better. Better than what? Well, better than they were. God is telling a story, and we are that many more chapters closer to the eucatastrophic denouement of His story. As we progress through His narrative, we should be able to tell what is going on. We should be reading with excitement, looking ahead at what is coming.

To say that Christianity is progressive is not to borrow from the secularists. The traffic actually goes the other way. Evolution is a Christian heresy—a twisting or a bending of this Christian idea of progress. Of course there is no way to account for progress in a cosmos without fixed standards, but the evolutionists try to anyway. As C.S. Lewis put it in his "Evolutionary Hymn,"

---

104 Arthur Herman, *The Idea of Decline in Western History* (New York: Free Press, 2007).

> Lead us, Evolution, lead us
> Up the future's endless stair;
> Chop us, change us, prod us, weed us.
> For stagnation is despair:
> Groping, guessing, yet progressing,
> Lead us nobody knows where.

When you don't know where you are going, you can always make good time. When survival is the only prize at the end of the process, evolution could end with a world full of three-foot-long cockroaches, and we would be forced to call it good. Like all heresies, progressive evolution has to live off a host, which in this case is the Christian faith. In the meantime, *oddly*, numerous Christians have abandoned this basic Christian narrative and have adopted the idea of decline. It consequently seems self-evident to many Christians that things are getting consistently worse and worse.

Let's run a little thought experiment, shall we? P.J. O'Rourke once quipped that he could refute those who didn't believe in progress in one word, that one word being *dentistry*. Let's add some other areas in which, taking an average, things are improving. Whether it is in standards of living or literacy or health, the last century has seen remarkable improvements. We can do this even while taking into account those portions of the globe that were run by homicidal lunatics as well as the cozy places of American academia that were dedicated to the defense of said lunatics. Remember that we are not comparing things to an ideal Platonic state, but rather comparing them to way they were *before*.

And we are not looking at history in five-year increments, but rather in five-hundred-year increments. I would rather be alive now than in 1512, and I would have preferred 1512 to 1012. After all, in 1512, I would have had the opportunity to buddy up with Luther, and in 1012, I would have been stuck as an advisor to Harold the Not Conqueror.

Now here is the thought experiment. If I say something like this in Christian circles, the response will come back that I am pointing to "earthly" improvements, not spiritual ones. Is this not a case of setting my mind on things below, clean contrary to Paul's admonition to the Colossians? Not really. As Yogi Berra once put it, you can observe a lot by just watching. You want spiritual things? How about the astonishing rate at which Africa, China, and South America are being brought to Christ? Philip Jenkins has made the (pretty surprising) case for this.[105] But it is only surprising to those who have adopted the non-Christian and unbelieving idea of decline.

This is why I say that this is not "an idea" (optimism) versus "the facts" (realistic pessimism). All facts are interpreted in accordance with a worldview system. And I am saying that the biblical worldview system requires us to believe that living water flows out from Ezekiel's temple until it brings life to the whole world, and healing to all the nations. I filter the evidence through *that* grid.

One last thing. It may be said that I am here evidencing a deficient sense of man's sinfulness. But I protest—as much as

---

105  See Phillip Jenkins, *The Next Christendom* (New York: Oxford University Press, 2011) and *The New Faces of Christianity* (New York: Oxford University Press, 2008).

I welcome criticism, this is mere abuse. I think a fair reading of how I look at the world will reveal that I believe that the supply of human and congressional follies are virtually endless. *Sin is a giant, sure enough.*

But when Joshua and Caleb countered the ten other spies, the point of disagreement between them was not over the size or reality of the Canaanite giants. It would have done the ten spies no good to claim that Joshua and Caleb had a "deficient view of giants." And many years later, David knew the size and power of Goliath as well as anyone.

To say that Christ has conquered sin and the devil does not require us to maintain that the sin was trivial and the devil a midget in order for us to keep our gospel "believable" to skeptical outsiders. Great views of sin should lead us to great views of salvation. Great but fearful views of sin can lead to the additional sin of hanging back, hesitant in unbelief. And because we do not label that unbelief as part of this sin, our views of sin are clearly not great *enough*.

Jesus Christ, Lord of the next Christendom, won a great victory before He was enthroned where He is currently enthroned, at the right hand of the Father. We do not honor that victory by acting as though it passed through history the same way Jesus passed through the wall of the upper room, without leaving a hole. No, He left a hole, all right. History has never been the same and can never be the same. Your great-great-grandchildren will live in a world that will be that much closer to the time when the leaves for the healing of the nations will be in the actual possession of every nation.

# 6

# FOR CHRISTENDOM

So I have been using the phrase mere Christendom a lot. What does the *mere* mean?

First we need to address what mere does not mean. And it does not mean "diluted." It does not mean Christendom Lite. It does not mean "faith-based" civilization, the same way you might have faith-based soup kitchens, with the content of the faith being diluted just enough to not bother those who are providing the secularist tax monies. If Christ is Lord, and He *is*, then those who believe that He is Lord should also think that it follows that He is the Lord of these United States and, going beyond our shores, that He is the Lord of every other place as well. Once this is accepted in multiple nations, in a formal and public way, you have the beginnings of the next Christendom.

So I do not mean a civilization is grounded on the Christian faith, but in such a way that keeps us from taking it "too seriously." People all know what happens when religiotards start taking their faith too seriously. Hands get chopped off, the woman caught in adultery—the one Christ forgave—is condemned at the appellate level, baptistic pastors are flogged for their incorrect exegesis of Col. 2:11, and so forth. That's what will happen, right? *Wrong*. Or, to be more accurate, mostly wrong.

But why do we think that, and why is it (just mostly) wrong? Often our baptistic brethren will lead the way in asking these questions, and it has to be said they have good historical reasons for being so jumpy.

We have to remember several things. First, history is messy, and when Christians have thrown other Christians into the slammer, sometimes the jailing Christians were at fault, other times the jailed ones were, and sometimes both. Sometimes the persecution was provoked by the one with the guns and keys, and other times it was provoked by the ones with nothing more than a talent for brinksmanship. For example, take Servetus coming to Geneva, with a "double-dog-dare-ya" attitude. And, speaking of Servetus, it should be mentioned that his execution was a brief ecumenical moment for a troubled Europe—Catholics, Lutherans, and Reformed all threw their hats in the air. Condemnations from this distance are cheap and easy for moderns to offer, and so we do, but it is not *approval* of the execution of that unfortunate heretic to note that you kind of had to have been there.

I need to look like I am changing the subject for a moment, but this appearance is illusory. When I made my peace with infant baptism about twenty-five years ago, I knew I had to find a way to account for the presence of baptized infidelity and, kicking it up a notch, baptized wickedness. You sometimes get those things, and you have to have a theological framework for dealing with them beforehand, one that takes biblical discipline seriously. But for the paedobaptist, that is not the real pastoral problem. You sometimes get baptized wickedness, *but you always get baptized immaturity.* Baptized immaturity is built right into the system, by definition. Peter Leithart points out that this is Yoder's problem with Constantine—he has no theological room to allow for such immaturity.[106]

We have to remember that when the modern era was forming, there was a battle for the soul of that modern era. It was not the case that "religion" fought itself to the point of exhaustion in the Thirty Years' War, decided to privatize itself in order to let the secularists run things, and since then the secularists had invented all these cool, modern gadgets. That would be a tad simplistic. The modern era was actually birthed by the Reformation, and the Enlightenment then hijacked it, claiming credit for a whole bunch of things it didn't really do. Anachronistic and self-serving claim-jumping is what it does best. Had the Enlightenment not happened, we

---

106  Peter Leithart, *Defending Constantine: The Twilight of an Empire and the Dawn of Christendom* (Downer's Grove, IL: InterVarsity Press, 2011).

would still have a recognizable modern era—just the same, only different.

This means that a return to Christendom does not entail a return to Geneva, circa A.D. 1590. It means that we are allowed to remember some of the things we have learned in the interim. I am simply insisting that we place the lessons we have learned in an explicitly Christ-honoring context and that we reject, throw away, and otherwise dispose of those bogus things we just *thought* we learned. An example of the former would be a true political space for true liberty of conscience—a development demonstrably grounded in Christian theology. An example of the latter would be the clear Darwinian idea that we are all nothing more than a raggle-taggle collection of protoplasm with no more rights than what the ruling classes decide we should have this coming week.

Now, one of the basic lessons we should have learned in the interim is this. The leaven works through the loaf slowly. The mustard seed grows slowly. The living water from Ezekiel's temple gets *gradually* deeper. But when doctrinaire Christians get power, one of their temptations is that they want to impose their whole system, down to the jots and tittles. We *must* refrain from doing this not because truth is relative, because it isn't, not because truth is a matter of community-perspective and there are multiple communities, for that is incoherent, but because Jesus Christ demands that we refrain.

I said above that the fear of Christians mistreating Christians was mostly wrong. It has been, and it will be, regrettably, *sometimes* right. The temptation mentioned in the previous paragraph is not universally resisted. But it ought to be— Christian maturity demands it. But if I grant that it will not be universally resisted, then why do I want to run the risk?

The answer is that we are not registering our wishes from some neutral zone. I am wishing for a civilization where— my critics would say—a baptist might be fined for failing to understand the covenant with Abraham. Right, but I am not wishing for this civilization from my seat on the balconies of Heaven. Rather I am wishing for it in a civilization where baptists are *currently* fined for not separating their garbage, fined for having the wrong kind of light bulb, fined for providing a baptist education to their homeschooled kids, and fined for holding Bible studies in residential neighborhoods that aren't zoned for that. In large part, I want out of this secularist paradise we are in because I think it is high time that we laid off the baptists.

I want to live in a baptized civilization. That is what I mean by mere Christendom. But this means, if I understand what I want, that I also want to live in the midst of baptized immaturity. If we are the Dufflepuds, and a glance at the national debt indicates that we most certainly are, then we have a long way to go. But if that is the raw material, what should you prefer? Wicked, infidel Dufflepuds or baptized and thoroughly exasperating Dufflepuds. I go with the latter.

So how will differing Christians get along? Isn't there a real danger of compromising our confession? This is another concern of the radical two-kingdoms advocates, such as Scott

Clark. He writes in *Tabletalk* that it would be a great loss to
water down our ecclesiastical identity through a shared notion of "Christian culture."[107] So many different issues con-
verge here that it will be necessary to spend a little bit of time
de-confusing them.

Clark's article concerns what to do with the pilgrims from
evangelicalism that may be making their way into confessional Reformed churches. "Upon arrival, the visitor is likely
to find new language and culture, that is, a new theology, piety, and practice."[108] Clark grants that the traffic is not exactly
heavy—evangelicals in North America number about sixty
million and there are less than a million members of confessional Reformed churches. But there *is* traffic, and Clark discusses what to do about it. Jumping to the end of the article,
Clark, to his credit, urges that these faithful Reformed believers decline to surrender their heritage, and that they "gently,
gradually, welcome" these pilgrims to the confessional tradition. Thus far, this is all to the good.

But there is a glitch. Knowing the particular kind of confessional tradition that passes muster with Clark, certain
comments he makes in the course of this article throw this
reviewer into a state of consternation.

"There remain, however, churches that not only trace their
roots to the Reformation but who also continue to believe
the same faith confessed by Calvin and his successors."[109]

---

107  R. Scott Clark, "Pilgrims (and Their Hosts)," *Tabletalk*, 34, no. 2 (February
2010): 76–77.
108  Ibid., 76.
109  Ibid., 77.

This will fly when you are dealing with refugees from pabulum churches who don't know the history or theology of the Reformation. A radical two-kingdom approach is something that someone can hold and still go to Heaven, obviously, but it most emphatically is not "the same faith confessed by Calvin and his successors." It is the same faith with bits and pieces of it, sure.

I'll bet that if you got Scott Clark and the great Puritan William Perkins in a battle-of-the-bands face off, and asked each of them to play that old fifties standard, *ordo salutis*, it would recognizably be the same song. But there are a whole bunch of *other* issues, issues that show up in virtually all the Reformed confessions, and that take up the lion's share of the Reformers' biographies, which, if you apply the acids of radical two-kingdom theology to them, just come apart in your hands.

"Now the confessional churches are isolated from both the old liberal mainline and the revivalist traditions."[110] This is because they are isolated from pretty much everybody, and this, unfortunately, includes isolation from *the cultural potency of Reformed theology and piety*. And that potency, incidentally, is one of the most obvious things about Reformed theology. The Reformed theology I have read and studied and loved built a great civilization. The Reformed theology of the truncated R2K brethren, consistently applied, would have trouble building a taco stand.

"If you found yourself in an intentionally historic, confessional Reformed congregation, you may have even done a

110  Ibid.

little time traveling to the seventeenth or even the sixteenth century."[111] Look. If you actually did some time travel to Geneva or Heidelberg or London or Wittenberg or Strasbourg in order to get the impression that Scott Clark is talking about, you would have to be given guided tours that kept you out of nine out of ten of those cities and out of 100 percent of the theological discussions. You would be given a guided tour of every sixteenth-century Potemkin village there was.

"It may take time for Americans raised on religious fast food to learn to enjoy a new diet, language and culture. If we try to become what the pilgrim has left behind, what use are we to the pilgrim? (Mt. 5:13)."[112] Clark describes evangelicals abandoning the fast food of revivalism, and it is an apt metaphor. But it is possible to abandon breakfast, lunch, and dinner at the Golden Arches without insisting that the only restaurant in the world with confessional food is a sushi bar in Escondido.

And it is here that Clark has gotten the picture exactly backward. As an evangelical and the son of an evangelical, allow me to give my *testimony*. I was part of the exodus from pop evangelicalism (not historic evangelicalism). I was sick of the cultural irrelevance and impotence of a simplistic "believe in Jesus, go to Heaven when you die, the Bible doesn't speak about anything else." I was sick of a pietism that couldn't find its way out of the prayer closet. I wanted to stop confessing that Jesus was Lord of an invisible seventeenth dimension somewhere. Why not here? Why not now? It was a long

111  Ibid.
112  Ibid.

story, but the trail to historic evangelicalism, God-honoring worship, and a culturally potent and world-transforming faith led me straight to the Reformed faith—the same faith that John Calvin and his successors confessed. Calvin preached to milkmaids, and Calvin wrote letters to princes. Calvin drafted catechisms, and he drafted ordinances for the city council. Calvin thought that the idea of a civil society without enforcement of the first table of the law was "preposterous." Calvin was a loyal son of Christendom, as am I.

Clark says that if the confessionally Reformed make the mistake of trying "to become what the pilgrim has left behind, what use are we to the pilgrim?" This is actually an outstanding question. Let me answer it for him. What he is arguing for—principled cultural irrelevance for Jesus—is *exactly* what I left behind, and I left it behind because historic Reformed believers taught me better. He has, *at this point*, abandoned the historic Reformed faith, and he has joined himself to the anabaptists and revivalists. I can describe it for him well—I grew up in that, and I know exactly what it is like.

In this modern "confessional" church, would they vote to ordain John Knox? Would they vote to ordain Martin Bucer? Would they vote to ordain John Calvin? Would they vote to ordain Abraham Kuyper? Would they vote to ordain Jonathan Edwards? Looking over that list, I would be able to vote for them, five for five. What would the radical two-kingdom advocates do? Treat them as pilgrims who needed to be taught some of the nuances of the true confessional tradition?

Returning to James Davison Hunter's *To Change the World*, we find another view of internalized religious culture—a theology of "faithful presence." He begins by making a strong connection between presence and place.

"Rather, in every instance, God's word was enacted and enacted in a particular place and time in history. In all, presence and place mattered decisively. Nowhere is this more evident than in the incarnation."[113] This is curious, because he leaves the point about place largely undeveloped. But the incarnate Christ is the universal particular, and this defines true globalism as well as true parochialism. It really does have ramifications for how local and particular love can be kept from tribalism or, at the terrible end, blood and soil idolatries, while at the same time not dissipating into the vague mist of globalizing bromides. I was sorry that Hunter didn't develop this more.

But because Jesus is Lord, and *only* because Jesus is Lord, I can love living in Latah County, here with my people, and also love the approach of the day in which all the nations are truly united—not in Turtle Bay, located in Manhattan, but in Jesus Christ, located at the right hand of the Father.

Hunter does say wonderful things, but he still can't let the clutch out. "Faithful presence means a constructive resistance that seeks new patterns of social organization that challenge, undermine, and otherwise diminish oppression, injustice, enmity, and corruption and, in turn, encourage harmony, fruitfulness and abundance, wholeness, beauty, joy, security, and

113  Hunter, 24.

well-being."[114] Okay, I'll bite. *Where* do oppression, injustice, etc., get challenged, undermined, and diminished? *Where* do wholeness, beauty, and joy take root? The point is clear enough—the rainbows appear in the sky, and the Smurfs come out to dance—but *when* will this happen? *Where* does it happen? On *what scale* does it happen?

This is important to mention because Hunter has already made it abundantly clear that it cannot be permitted to happen *too much*, for if that occurred we would find that we had a little too much triumphalism and Constantinian shalom going along with it.

Previously, Hunter had made a point of urging us to remember that a bunch of our work in this world is not in any way establishing the kingdom. But then, curiously, he says this: "All of this has resulted in a peculiar approach to faith and vocation. For generations of faithful Evangelicals and Fundamentalists, vocation in the secular world was at best a necessary evil. To the extent that work had 'kingdom significance,' it was as a platform for evangelism."[115]

Rather than saying "necessary evil," it would be more accurate to say that evangelicals and fundamentalists have thought of work as some kind of a neutral good, but one that has no direct kingdom significance. They said this because of a debilitating eschatology, which is exactly the same reason that Hunter has argued for precisely the same kind of thing.

114  Ibid., 247–48.
115  Ibid., 248–49.

But because God has placed eternity in our hearts, *we are not built* to relate our labors to nothing much in particular. If our hedge-planting, plank-sanding, columns-of-numbers-counting, ship-building, logging, mining, fishing, legislating, architecting, and more are not examples of kingdom work, then we will come to relate it somehow to that which *is* kingdom work. Hunter relates it to evangelism and faithful testimony just as the evangelicals and fundamentalists do, with the only difference being that he is intellectually sophisticated enough to talk about it in terms like "faithful presence" and "shalom" instead of doing it the old school way by leaving tracts in laundromats. But the same basic move of creating eternal significance is occurring.

But thinking *missional shalom* instead of *evangelistic soul-winning* only makes you cooler, not more effective at it.

In his last chapter, "Toward a New City Commons," Hunter takes Jeremiah 29:4–7 as his key text, wherein the Jews in exile were told to seek the peace of the city they would inhabit for a time.

> Clearly it would have been justifiable for the Jews to be hostile to their captors. It also would have been natural enough for them to withdraw from engaging the world around them. By the same token, it would have been easy for them to simply assimilate with the culture that surrounded them. Any of these three options made sense in human terms. But God was calling them to something different—not to be defensive against, isolated from, or

absorbed into the dominant culture, but to be faithfully present within it.[116]

Yea and amen to that. But what happened *then*?

Then was the king exceeding glad for him, and commanded that they should take Daniel up out of the den. So Daniel was taken up out of the den, and no manner of hurt was found upon him, because he believed in his God. And *the king commanded*, and they brought those men which had accused Daniel, and *they cast them into the den of lions, them, their children, and their wives; and the lions had the mastery of them, and brake all their bones in pieces or ever they came at the bottom of the den.* Then king Darius wrote unto all people, nations, and languages, that dwell in all the earth; Peace be multiplied unto you. *I make a decree, That in every dominion of my kingdom men tremble and fear before the God of Daniel: for he is the living God, and steadfast for ever, and his kingdom that which shall not be destroyed, and his dominion shall be even unto the end.* He delivereth and rescueth, and he worketh signs and wonders in heaven and in earth, who hath delivered Daniel from the power of the lions. So this Daniel prospered in the reign of Darius, and in the reign of Cyrus the Persian. (Dan. 6:23–28, emphasis mine)

So Darius, like Constantine, had a few rough edges. Come to think of it, Nebuchadnezzar had a few rough edges, too.

Then Nebuchadnezzar spake, and said, Blessed be the God of Shadrach, Meshach, and Abednego, who hath

116  Ibid., 277.

sent his angel, and delivered his servants that trusted
in him, and have changed the king's word, and yield-
ed their bodies, that they might not serve nor worship
any god, except their own God. *Therefore I make a decree,*
*That every people, nation, and language, which speak any*
*thing amiss against the God of* Shadrach, Meshach, and
Abednego, *shall be cut in pieces, and their houses shall be*
*made a dunghill: because there is no other God that can de-*
*liver after this sort.* Then the king promoted Shadrach,
Meshach, and Abednego, in the province of Babylon.
(Dan. 2:28–30, emphasis mine)

I would counsel extreme caution. Do you see the sorts of
excesses that faithful presence can lead to? I mean, political
opponents *and* their wives and children fed to ravenous lions?
Theological critics, who were simply publishing their honest opinions about Daniel's God in respectable and refereed
theological journals, getting cut into pieces and their houses
made into dunghills? I mean, this is a dangerous business, this
faithful presence stuff. You have to watch your step *constantly.*
If you are too faithful, you might *win,* and that would set the
cat among the pigeons.

Hunter is calling in this chapter for a "new city commons."
In order to have a commons, you must have something in
common. In order to have that commons, you must have a
new city. What is the nature of Hunter's new city? Well, according to Hunter's description, it is a pluralistic one.

What is 'new' in the new city commons? Against the
dominant liberal modernist notion that the public sphere

is constituted by a diversity of autonomous and unen-
cumbered individuals, in this view there is a recognition
that public diversity–whose focal metaphor is the city–is
also defined collectively by multiple traditions and communities. Needless to say, some of these are very different from, if not hostile to, the community of Christian
believers. But even where there is disagreement, tension,
and conflict, there is also a recognition that there are
common goods that communities of Christians, draw-
ing on the resources of their tradition, must still hold up,
pursue, work at, foster, and practice. *In short, commitment
to the new city commons is a commitment of the community
of faith to the highest ideals and practices of human flourish-
ing in a pluralistic world.*[117]

This is simply amazing. In short, instead of individual-based
pluralism, we now have community-based pluralism. But the
theological name for pluralism is *polytheism*. Instead of household Baals, Hunter wants us to configure the new city commons in such a way as to accommodate the Baals of every shire
and valley. But how can Christians make *principled* peace with
any other gods? Jesus is Lord, and His claims are total. Our
assigned task was to take every thought captive, and to throw
down every high thing that sets itself against the knowledge of
God (2 Cor. 10:5). Isn't that what we were told to do?

The Bible describes a new city and a new city commons,
but it is nothing like this. There are no other gods in it, for
starters. "And the city had no need of the sun, neither of the
moon, to shine in it: for the glory of God did lighten it, and

117   Ibid., 279, emphasis his.

the Lamb is the light thereof. And the nations of them which are saved shall walk in the light of it: and the kings of the earth do bring their glory and honour into it" (Rev. 21:23–24).

Why is this book so popular in conservative Christian circles? We don't have to read any further. This book has been well received because, at the end of the day, Hunter lets us off the hook. And we love *nothing* more than a little bit of being let off the hook.

God has fashioned the world in such a way that we always have to come down to the *point*. However much we might want to obscure the issues, however much we might build great universities with trained brains to cover everything in a dark mist, however much we reward those pundits who make ample room for our lusts and opinions, at the end of the day, we have to decide if we are going to do it God's way or not.

Everything we do must be done to the glory of God. If a Christian argues in favor of a certain form of government, then he must, in the final analysis, argue that God *wants* him to argue in favor of that form of government. If God doesn't want that, then why is he doing it? If God does want it, how does he know? And if, in his system of theology, God doesn't give a rip, why does he call his system of theology *Christian*?

So there we are. Say, just for a random example, a Christian wants to argue in favor of a secular government. I know, crazy talk, but sometimes you have to use extreme examples to make a point. That Christian has to say either that God doesn't want government to be secular, but that he, the secular Christian, wants it anyway, which is disobedience, or that God *does* want secular government, and "let me show you all the places in the Bible where God warns kings and princes about the importance of making sure they *never* acknowledge Him in any of their ways," which is exegetically incoherent, or "let me show you from the Bible that some form of Deism is true," which is false.

Convoluted political theology doesn't like to be pinned down this way, but this is what it amounts to. If Baal is god, follow him. If Yahweh is God, follow Him. There are no third-party movements on Mount Carmel. Everybody is in the game, and there are no sidelines. So what's it gonna be?

Christians who argue for a secular public square are caught on the horns of a dilemma. Either Jesus wants this or He doesn't. Or maybe He doesn't care. If He doesn't want it, then why do they? If He does, then are they not advocating a civil arrangement based on the will of the Lord, which would be a theocracy? And if He doesn't care, then that means, incidentally, that it would be *okay* for us to build a theocracy. I mean, He didn't say we *couldn't*.

When we are talking about a theocracy in the abstract, we are not yet talking about the content of the laws, only that the laws are based on the will of God. Biblical law, rightly understood, would *not* be draconian, but that needs to be discussed in its place. Right now, the question is whether or not public morality needs to be grounded in the will of God or not.

So let's take this a step further. If the laws are not based on the will of God, but rather on the will of the people, Demos, then what happens when a large majority of the people think that the laws should be based on the will of a god? This is precisely the dilemma that democracy faces in the Middle East. The president of Turkey has said that democracy is like a street car—you ride it until your stop. *Then you get off.* What happens when an Islamic state forms as a result of democratic processes? What happens when Hamas actually wins the election in Gaza, and they didn't do it by cheating?

In effect, Demos the capricious god gives way to another god. But on secularist principles, why would Demos not have the right to abdicate like this? Who says that Demos can't abdicate?

When a Christian secularist looks at this kind of scenario, if Demos is the final word, then cannot Demos vote itself out of having the final word? Can it not enthrone Allah? If Allah is not the true God and does not exist, can it not, at any rate, enthrone the mullahs?

Or what about Jesus? On what basis could a Christian secularist object to an election that voted in Jesus as Lord? He could do it only by saying that Jesus refused to be nominated, and then point to a text that showed us how Jesus required our civil affairs to be arranged and that He was particularly insistent that we be sure to leave Him out of it. But the whole point for the secularist is that there is no such text, which, ironically, opens the door for a democratic Christian republic.

Now of course, I believe that Jesus is already the crowned King, not an elected president, and that the Great Commission requires us to proclaim that the coronation has already happened. Jesus is not running for anything, and we do not "make" Him anything. He is the Lord of lords, the King of kings, and the President of presidents, and there is nothing whatever that we can do about it. It is already the case. The world will gradually come to recognize this, and will become Christian, and this is good news indeed. This is *the* good news.

And this, incidentally, is why I believe that Christian republics and commonwealths are formed by preaching, baptizing, and discipleship and not by campaigning, legislating, pundit-blogging, and so on. This gospel work will have political *results*, but it is not politically established. The magistrate is a necessary part of the process, but only as a servant to the gospel. The magistrate must wear Christ's livery, and not the other way around.

So here are the options:

1. Jesus doesn't care whether or not nations are explicitly Christian.

2. Jesus is opposed to nations being explicitly Christian.

3. Jesus wants nations to be explicitly Christian.

And here should be our responses to these possibilities:

1. Well, if Jesus doesn't care, that means we have the right to care. So let's make this a Christian nation, shall we?

2. Let's have a Bible study and find out why "disciple the nations" really means "don't disciple the nations, whatever you do."

3. Yes, Lord.

# 7

# SOME CHRISTENDOM MYTHS

## BUT WHAT ABOUT . . .?

As has already been said, by *mere Christendom*, I mean a public
and formal recognition of the authority of Jesus Christ that
repudiates the principles of secularism and that avoids both
hard sectarianism and easy latitudinarianism. Easier said than
done, but there it is. That is what we have to do, and we have
to do it because secularism has run its course and does not
have the wherewithal to resist the demands of radical Islam.

It is possible to argue for this without supporting an "established church," which—in the form of tax revenues—I do
*not* support. But in order for this to happen at all, the Church
must be established in the sense that the magistrate has the

responsibility to recognize her and to listen to her. The magistrate himself has the responsibility, as a public figure, in the discharge of his office, to believe in Jesus, Lord of Heaven and earth.

How this could possibly be done is quite tricky, but again, there it is. Different nations would receive "baptism" differently, but in our political tradition it would be by means of something like referencing the Lordship of Jesus Christ in the Constitution. That would make me happy, for starters. In short, I am arguing for a Christian America. I am not arguing for an America that is *nominally* Christian. I am arguing for this because Jesus rose from the dead, and this trumps any briefs that the ACLU might be able to file.

We have been so well catechized by our secularist masters that the mere assertion of this causes us to start freaking out, anticipating a regime of Reformed ayatollahs, ready to chop off infidel heads at the slightest provocation. Let us leave aside for a moment the fact that this is exactly the kind of rule we will get if we don't discover something with enough backbone to withstand radical Islam. But even with that concern, we still have to answer the worries caused by the secularist catechism.

They have told us, *ad nauseam*, that our people were racked with bloody religious strife, back in the times of the Thirty Years' War, and when we had exhausted ourselves fighting over arcane religious dogmas, the secular state finally arose, and delivered us all from this kind of folly forever. These are the gods who brought us out of the land of Egypt. Yay.

SOME CHRISTENDOM MYTHS                    161

The problem with this take is that it is simply not true. That fighting was actually *caused* by the rise of the secular state, and was not in any meaningful sense what our phrase "a religious war" brings to mind. If it really had been pure religious strife, then what are we to make of the Catholic–Protestant alliances in it, and in the fact of Catholics fighting Catholics?

This is not to say that religious conflict is an impossibility—people are people, sinners are sinners, and one of the things we do is fight. But the notion that secularism has any virtue in it capable of stopping our tendency to bloodletting is beyond ludicrous. Consider the twentieth century, the century of secularism, the century of blood. If we didn't know better, we might say that the twentieth century was straight out of the book of Revelation, with blood up to the horses' bridles.

Here is a thought experiment for you. Take a couple of princes from the seventeenth century, one Catholic and one Protestant, and both of them experienced soldiers. Show them, in a vision, the battle of the Somme, the bombing of Dresden, the battle of Midway, the Great Leap Forward, the gulags of communism, and the two atomic bombs dropped on Japan. These men would be, in turns, appalled, thrilled, horrified, and appalled some more. But they wouldn't laugh at you until you mentioned that all this was a small price to pay for the deliverance from blood that it was providing for us.

Why do we believe things like the ludicrous memes that teach us that secularism delivered us from bloodshed? Among other things, a meme is a little bit of a verbal virus that gets passed around in a culture, like the common cold. After it gets passed around enough, people start to think it is the received wisdom. That said, here are seven memes that are common in our culture and have been used mightily to keep Christians in their place. Or, to return to the virus metaphor, the point of them is to hamper the ethos of Christians in public debate by ensuring that they are the ones who always have the sniffles and red noses.

After each meme, I have included the *briefest* of replies to each, all while expressing the desire that somebody would write a book on each one of these.

*1. The Crusades were totally uncalled for.*

The Crusades were actually a long overdue defensive reaction to many years of Muslim belligerence, militarism, aggressiveness, and provocation. If a "crusade" is an unprovoked military attack on religious grounds, then we need to start speaking of the Muslim Crusades. One could, however, criticize Christian Europe for being so slow to respond. There were, of course, problems with the Crusades caused by some Roman Catholic errors (e.g., crusading as a form of penance), and there was more than a little bit of papal aggrandizement that caused problems for Protestants later, but with regard to the basic political issues, the Crusades were entirely justified.

*2. The battle between Galileo and the Church was a battle between science and faith.*

The actual lesson of the Galileo debacle is that when the Church uncritically accepts the "best science of the day," as

they did with Aristotelian philosophy, and as many are doing
today with evolutionary thought, the results are usually disas-
trous. That battle was not between faith and science, but rather between the old science and the new science, with many
adherents of the old science doing their best to illustrate Max
Planck's dictum "science advances funeral by funeral."

*3. The Salem Witch Trials were an example of typical Puritan
intolerance.*

What actually went down was this. The charter for Massachusetts had been revoked in 1684 by King James II, who appointed Sir Edmond Andros as governor. Andros abolished
the Massachusetts General Court and imposed Episcopalian-
ism on the colony. In 1689, the colonists received word that the
king had been removed in the Glorious Revolution of 1688,
and so they promptly ousted Governor Andros. This left the
colony without any legally constituted government. Increase
Mather was sent to England to obtain a new charter from
King William. While he was away, the court cases piled up because the authorities had no basis for action; they had no legal
government. While he was gone, the witchcraft accusations
broke out in Salem (in February of 1692), and the officials in
the colony had no legal means to deal with them. The hysteria gathered steam, and the number of the accused exceeded
seventy by that June. When Mather returned at the tail end
of this hysteria (in the middle of May) with the charter (and
the new governor, William Phips), they were confronted with
a huge backlog of cases, including the Salem witch cases. The
new governor appointed a special court in Salem, which *the*

*clergymen did not control,* and the trials and executions began. *The trials themselves were egregious.* Shortly after he appointed the special court, Governor Phips asked for the counsel of the area ministers. Their "Return" to him was dated June 15, 1692, and was drafted by Cotton Mather and signed by a number of the ministers. They *opposed* the admission of spectral evidence and evidence by ordeal, and they urged that in cases like this "there is need of a very critical and exquisite caution." By October, Governor Phips was persuaded to put a halt to the witch trials. But by then, the damage was done and Puritans everywhere were tagged with a guilt that their leaders had in the main conscientiously opposed.[118]

*4. The rise of the secular Enlightenment saved us all from endless religious bloodletting.*

Since secularism took over from the bad old religious bigots who used to kill scores and scores of people, we have since that time had a long millennium of sunshine and glittery rainbows, in which only scores of *millions* of people have been slaughtered. We celebrate this deliverance of ours and bow our heads in gratitude.

*5. Darwinian evolution is the truth.*

Darwinian evolution is actually the funniest thing I ever heard of. It is so dumb that the average Christian needs at least three years of graduate study from white-haired profs to get adjusted to it.

---

118   See Chris Schlect, "Salem in 1692" Parts I, II, and III in *Credenda/Agenda*, 7, Nos. 1, 2, and 3 respectively (undated): 23, 23, 23, respectively.

*6. Biblical faith stifles and deadens the aesthetic soul.*

I will not say much here, except to note that I do not believe that the builders of Salisbury Cathedral, the composer of the *Brandenburg Concertos*, the painter of *The Night Watch*, or the writer of *Paradise Lost*, have anything to apologize for in the thin shade of Kanye West, John Cage, Jackson Pollock, Walter Gropius, or Barry Manilow.

*7. America was a secular nation in its founding.*

Our Constitution was established in the year of our Lord 1789. We were one of the last nations of the first Christendom to be founded, and we have had our share of scamps and hypocrites (which is actually a prerequisite for even *being* a nation of Christendom), but at the same time, we were truly founded as a Christian republic. We are in the grip of apostasy fever now, but we weren't then. To go along with a lie about our founding is to capitulate to a lie about our current apostastic monkeyshines. And we should all resolve to learn more about what *those* are.

## THE T-WORD

It is not possible to suggest such things without those trained and catechized by our secularist age getting frightened. One of the great bugbear words is the very scary *theocracy*. Jason Stellman argues that theocracy requires two components—rule and realm—and he defines a theocracy as "an arrangement in which God provides for his covenant people a distinct land in which they are to serve Him as His loyal subjects."[119]

119 Stellman, *Dual Citizens*, xix.

By this definition, our first parents lived in a theocracy because God was worshiped, and they lived within the realm that He gave them. "This means that God's reign over pre-fallen man was a dominion that included a *domain*, a rule that included a *realm*—namely, the garden of Eden."[120] He argues that this theocracy continued until the Fall. "Once man declared his rebellious sovereignty, his kingdom became distinct from God's kingdom, causing an unnatural separation between cult and culture."[121] Notice the assumption that the separation was successful in this at least—that man had wrested culture away from God and made it his own realm.

Because the patriarchs did not have such a land, they served God in a situation where there was a separation between cult and culture. "The situation of the patriarchs before the giving of the law, therefore, can be characterized as *pilgrim politics*, a term that highlights their status not as a triumphant theocratic army but as 'resident aliens' and 'tolerated sojourners' whose inheritance was not yet a reality."[122] The shape of culture therefore belonged to the unbelievers outside, the worship of God proper belonged to the believers within the patriarchal orbit.

Under the law of Moses, the people of Israel came back under a theocracy, with both God's rule and God's realm defined. "Like Adam but unlike the patriarchs, the people of Israel under the Mosaic covenant were both cultically *and*

120  Ibid., xix.
121  Ibid., xx.
122  Ibid., xxi.

culturally distinct from all other nations on the earth."[123] But this only applied *within* the borders of Israel. This is how Stellman accounts for Solomon's being able to have friendly dealings with the king of Tyre and the queen of Sheba.[124] "Did Solomon not realize that these were heathen rulers?"[125] It also seems to account for God's instruction through Jeremiah (Jer. 29:4–7) to seek the welfare of heathen Babylon.[126] So with this understanding, Israel functioned like a theocracy within its borders, and like a pilgrim nation in its foreign policy.

"And what determines whether God's people are a theocracy or a band of pilgrims? The answer is simple: *a distinct land*. A theocracy, as I pointed out above, always has a geographical element to it."[127] What does this do for our day? Under the new covenant, our "situation [is] more like that of the patriarchs under the Abrahamic covenant than that of Israel under the Mosaic covenant."[128] Got all that? We had a theocracy in Eden. It was lost in the Fall, and the patriarchs were a pilgrim Church. Theocracy was restored under Moses, and then abandoned for the new covenant.

We, therefore, must come to the New Testament for instruction on two things. The first would be how God desires to be worshiped under the new covenant, and then, as a completely

---

123  Ibid., xxii.
124  Ibid., xxii.
125  Ibid., xxiii.
126  Ibid., xxiii.
127  Ibid., xxiv.
128  Ibid., xxv.

distinct matter, how to live as pilgrims in the midst of a hostile or indifferent unbelieving culture. But until the Last Day, that outside unbelieving culture is a fixed given and will not be fundamentally changed. According to Stellman, we will always need instruction on how to live there as *pilgrims*.

> Civil institutions that existed in New Testament times, such as marriage (1 Cor. 7:27), parenthood (Col. 3:20–21), slavery (1 Cor. 7:21), and government (Rom. 13:1ff), were considered legitimate expressions of the kingdom of man, and participation in them was not ruled out by one's membership in the kingdom of Christ. However, though membership in the body of Christ did not alter the *fact* that believers in the early church participated in these things, it most certainly altered the *way* in which they participated in them.[129]

If we cash this out, this is what we see. "In non-theocratic contexts, where God's people were pilgrims without an earthly land (such as the patriarchs, Israel and Judah in exile, and the new covenant church), the religious sphere is distinct from the cultural sphere."[130]

What are we to say to all this? The first thing to note about this setup is that it appears to me to be internally consistent. The thesis statement (theocracy requires land) is one that can be held up against the situation of God's people in various times and places, and there tested. Unfortunately, it only

---

129  Ibid., xxvi.
130  Ibid., xxvii.

passes the first round of tests. If we look closer at Abraham and Daniel, say, the thesis starts to come apart in our hands.

Take just two examples of what ought to be an occasion for pure pilgrim politics, but which do not appear to have been used that way.

> And when Abram heard that his brother was taken captive, he armed his trained servants, born in his own house, three hundred and eighteen, and pursued them unto Dan. And he divided himself against them, he and his servants, by night, and smote them, and pursued them unto Hobah, which is on the left hand of Damascus. And he brought back all the goods, and also brought again his brother Lot, and his goods, and the women also, and the people . . . . And Melchizedek king of Salem brought forth bread and wine: and he was the priest of the most high God. And he blessed him, and said, Blessed be Abram of the most high God, possessor of heaven and earth: And blessed be the most high God, which hath delivered thine enemies into thy hand. And he gave him tithes of all. (Gen. 14:14–16, 18–20)

Looks like a triumphant theocratic army to me.

> Then Nebuchadnezzar spake, and said, Blessed be the God of Shadrach, Meshach, and Abednego, who hath sent his angel, and delivered his servants that trusted in him, and have changed the king's word, and yielded their bodies, that they might not serve nor worship any god, except their own God. Therefore I make a decree, That every people, nation, and language, which speak any thing amiss against the God of Shadrach, Meshach,

and Abednego, shall be cut in pieces, and their houses shall be made a dunghill: because there is no other God that can deliver after this sort. Then the king promoted Shadrach, Meshach, and Abednego, in the province of Babylon. (Dan. 2:28–30)

In short, faithfulness on the part of *pilgrims* is frequently honored by God, and it is honored by Him via cultural victories, and cultural transformations within those cultures operative *outside* the pilgrim band. Above we see a military victory won by a pilgrim army and a massive political victory won by some pilgrim advisors. When pilgrims participate in their surrounding culture and they do so in a different *way* (as Stellman acknowledges they do), what should they do when God gives them favor in the eyes of the leaders of that surrounding culture?

There are four other things to note. The first is that Stellman wrongly assumes that Gentile = nonbeliever. This is a common mistake, but if you remove this particular error from Stellman's argument, his whole case collapses. In the Old Covenant era, there was no obligation to become a Jew in order to be put right with God. It was not comparable to the believer/unbeliever grid that we have today. All men today are called to repent and believe in Christ. The gospel brings a universal call with it. But there was no Great Commission telling the Jews to bring the whole world into Israel, and this was not because all Gentiles had been written off. This is why we see faithful Gentiles like Melchizedek, Jethro, Naaman, the inhabitants of Nineveh, Job, and every faithful

Gentile who ever came to pray to Yahweh in the Court of the
Gentiles. The old covenant Temple was a house of prayer *for
all nations*. But if this is acknowledged (and I think it must
be acknowledged), it plays old Harry with Stellman's entire
argument.

Second, I am interested in his assertion about the need for
land in order for a theocracy to exist, although I am dubi-
ous about its creating an obligation to swear off theocracy.
Couldn't it go the other way? I would say that if the claims
of Christ are total, then theocracy means, of necessity, that
God is claiming (and promising) the *land*. Stellman is arguing from *no land* to *no theocracy*. Why not argue from *theocracy* to *let's pray to God for the land*? And I would throw a
glorious promise into this particular mix: "Children, obey
your parents in the Lord: for this is right. Honour thy father
and mother; (which is the first commandment with promise;)
That it may be well with thee, *and thou mayest live long on the
earth*" (Eph. 6:1–3, emphasis mine). Moses gave Israel what
Stellman would call a theocratic promise, and it was a promise connected to *land* (Deut. 5:16). Paul picks up that same
promise, treats it as a continuing promise, and cheerfully applies it to a bunch of Gentile Ephesian kids, and—consistent
with the promise—applies it to territory, to the earth. In fact,
he applies it to a great deal more territory than was involved
in the first iteration of the promise at Sinai. So I would say
that we have land the same way Israel did right after Joshua
crossed the Jordan, before Jericho fell. Was Israel a theocracy
in the wilderness? No land, no more permanent territory than

Abraham had. They lived in tents just like Abraham did. And
when they crossed the Jordan, they only had a few acres and
the rest of the land by promise, just like we do. They were not
yet cultivating all the vineyards, but that didn't matter. They
had the *promise* of land, just like we do.

Third, Stellman (unlike his hypothetical friend the really
consistent amillennialist) cannot really live by these principles. He writes, "While Christians would certainly agree that
many divisions have been unnecessary and wrong (such as
racial divisions), some distinctions must be maintained."[131]
Now wait a minute. Assume a church that keeps ungodly racial divisions out of its membership, as I am sure Stellman's
church did. On what basis could someone from that church
tell the unbelieving culture outside that her ethnic discrimina-
tions have been "unnecessary" and "wrong"? Wrong by what
standard? Unnecessary by what standard? Suppose we are
dealing with the kind of culture I grew up in, where schools
and restaurants and so forth were divided according to race.
I could, on Stellman's principles, argue and vote against this
kind of thing personally, but only in my own name. I could
not do so because this was "*the* Christian position." It would
have to be just me and my sensibilities. Not only so, but a
fellow member of my congregation could be an ardent seg-
regationist on the same principles. And we would be allowed
to derive those sensibilities from nowhere in particular, which
would lead to certain embarrassments in the Q&A session.

131  Ibid., xvii.

This leads to the last point—the distinction that Stellman wants to make between the Church and the individual Christian. In other words, he wants to say that his position does not prevent him from taking a stand against the Holocaust or against racial discrimination (as above). But I have no doubt that Stellman would indeed take a stand against great social evils. He just wouldn't be able to tell us why—or the most he could say is that as an individual Christian he was *allowed* to take this stand. But are there any cultural issues that require Christians to take a stand *as Christians*, in the name of Jesus? When I give a cup of cold water in Christ's name, in order for this to count as something done in His name, must it be on church property? (Mark 9:41) Must it be from the church drinking fountain?

## WAS AMERICA REALLY CHRISTIAN AT THE FOUNDING?

I've already briefly touched on the idea that the United States was established as a secular republic, but let me delve a little deeper into that myth.

Darryl Hart discusses the famous American trope, "a city on a hill," lifted from the Sermon on the Mount in a sermon by John Winthrop and by countless tub-thumping American politicos since. He discusses the development of this idea throughout American history, distinguishes between the optimistic postmillennial Americans and the pessimistic premillennialists, and then discusses Augustine's distinction between the two cities, the City of Man and the City of God.

He also shows that both Luther and Calvin interpreted the phrase "city on a hill" in ecclesiastical terms.[132]

There are two comments to make here. The first is that firmer distinctions must be made between the robustly Christian vision of the early fathers like Winthrop and the anemic optimism of their pre–World War I descendants. There is a vast canyon between the early postmillenialists, who believed that the gospel preached would bring the nations to Christ, and the pale, washed-out optimisms of foreign policy dreamers two centuries later. Hart is quite right that Massachusetts Bay Colony was "an effort to perpetuate Christendom."[133] But this effort stands alongside countless other variants of Christendom, and has *nothing* at all to do with secularized "Christendom," a "Protestantism without God."[134] There *were* problems with the New England effort, chief among them impatience and over-reaching, but these problems have little or nothing in common with the vague, gaseous uplift that the mainline denominations were peddling several centuries later.

The second comment is this: Hart relies on Augustine and cites Luther and Calvin on the "city on the hill" being the Church, but I suspect his application misses the point. All three of these gentlemen had very decided views on the governmental distinction that needed to be maintained between the Church and the state. But all three of them were also

132  Hart, *A Secular Faith*, 35 ff.
133  Ibid., 38.
134  Ibid., 45.

living in a time when the magistrate, dirty hands and all, still confessed Christ, and was still willing to listen to the Church when the Church spoke. Whether we are talking about Augustine and the Donatists, or Luther and the Peasants, or Calvin and Servetus, it is very clear that the division between Church and state was not as *tidy* in their minds as it appears to be in Hart's. My point is not to praise or blame these men in these instances, which can be done elsewhere. My point is more obvious—that if someone suggested to Luther or Calvin or Augustine that a rising candidate for emperor named Julian the Apostate appeared to be quite a fine fellow, classically educated and all, and his campaign literature is quite glossy, *none* of the three would respond with, "You know, *that* is a secular, political matter. Doesn't really concern me." Not even close.

## BACK TO THEOCRACY AND SECULARISM

One of the problems with using Constantine as a marker is that there is a tendency to anachronism, attributing to him any subsequent malfeasance on the part of Christians in power. But the Constantinian settlement was, by and large, a tolerant one. Lactantius, the early Church father who tutored Constantine's children, was an apologist for this kind of toleration, which, in his day, was a toleration of pagans.

But there is a distinction between toleration of the views held by others and toleration as an absolute desideratum. The former is crucial to every form of civilized society. Constantine let pagans continue to be pagans, and to think like pagans, and he let them continue to serve in the army (for example), but at the same time, Constantine ended the pagan sacrifices—a momentous step and foundational to all true religious liberty.

This distinction is necessary because at a certain level, the whole society has to decide whether to go this way or that way. For example, democracy does not mean that everybody votes for president, and the winner gets to be president 57 percent of the time while the loser only gets to be president on Tuesdays, Thursdays, and Saturdays. It is not like a custody battle. The public sacrifices for the whole society either have to be performed or not. The public square cannot be a pantheon—for if it is, then the state is god, and that is idolatry. Calling it secularism doesn't fix it.

There must be a God over all. That God may tell us not to hassle the people who don't believe in Him, and that is precisely what the triune God does tell us. In this mere Christendom I am talking about (you know, the idyllic one, down the road), Muslims could come from other lands and live peaceably, they could buy and sell, write letters to the editor, own property, have that property protected by the cops, and worship Allah in their hearts and homes. What they could not do is argue that minarets have the same rights of public expression that church bells do. The public space would belong to Jesus.

Our secular gods promised to do exactly this kind of thing, saying that if we kept this public space "neutral" (as *they* defined neutral), then we all would be allowed to do our own thing on our own time. But this secularism is teetering and is clearly displaying its hostility to the Christian faith. What I am saying here is that an explicitly Christian settlement would do a better job of protecting the true rights of Muslims and secularists than secularists do in protecting the rights of Christians.

The argument goes this way. If I wanted Muslims to have the right to refuse baptism (which I would certainly want), then I would have to argue that case in the name of Jesus and from the Bible. Obviously, I think that it can be done. But if I wanted to argue from the premises of secularism that all of us are anything more than meat, bones, and protoplasm, where do I go to make the argument? The implications of a godless universe have worked their way into the structure of our laws, and it is not too long afterward that the darkness falls. And it won't be the kind of night that you can dance away.

When tolerance becomes a universal virtue, suspended upon its own air hook and nothing else, then you come to think you can't say *no* to virtually anything—including those things which will issue a fatwa against your silly views of tolerance. The universally tolerant do say *no* to one thing, however, and that is to any idea of Christendom. If you mention sharia law, they will talk about the rich cultural diversity that is found in certain parts of Ohio. But if you mention biblical theocracy, as being perhaps more attractive in *other* parts of Ohio, you will find these folks with heads between their knees, breathing into paper bags in preparation for writing hysterical letters to the editor. This is because universal toleration is suicidal. In Proverbs, Wisdom says that all who hate her love death (Prov. 8:36), *and they really do*.

Our *fin de siècle* secularism is fully prepared to embrace that which will destroy it pronto and to shun as a menace that faith which actually invented true toleration.

But I propose a contest. Let's build an altar of stones, an altar of absolute toleration. Let's have ACLU lawyers dance around it until noon, cutting themselves with knives and hitting themselves on the head with briefcases. Let us build another altar, and ask Elijah to stretch out his hands toward Heaven and call upon Yahweh. The God that answers with a truly free and tolerant society . . . He is God. Let us serve Him.

# CHRISTENDOM QUESTIONS

We now have to put a few nuts and bolts on our project so that it can support our claims. Our tire of Christendom needs a few lug nuts, lest it fall off. Here are some fundamental principles, in response to some basic questions, which must underlie any workable and Protestant notion of "mere Christendom."

## NATURAL LAW?

Let me see if I can do something to simplify the idea of natural law or, as I would prefer to state it, natural revelation.

A couple of young brothers go home after school, accompanied by a couple of their unbelieving friends. When they get to the house, they find it clean and in good order. There

are some beautiful paintings on the wall, the work of the boys'
mother. On the counter is a tray of brownies, still warm. This
is natural law.

On the fridge is a note from mom, telling the boys to help
themselves to the brownies and, after they have done so,
would they please help her out by carrying a desk upstairs, a
desk she scored that morning in a yard sale. After that, they
can do whatever—study, go play ball, whatever they want to
do. That is special revelation.

There are three basic ways to screw this up. One way is
to separate the two forms of communication and focus your
attention on only one of them. The second way is to focus on
the other one. The third way is to accept both forms of revelation, but to treat them as the work of two different mothers.
The normal way to respond, the way her sons do, is by accepting all of it as coming from her, each according to its nature
and all part of a well-integrated home life.

If their unbelieving friends argue with them about it, it
doesn't bother the boys. They know who cooked the brownies,
and they know they can eat the brownies because the note
said they could, and they are also glad that there are brownies
there to eat—they don't have to settle for eating the note.

To accept the reality of natural law or revelation is not to
create an automatic dualism. The fact that some others have
done this is evidence of dualistic *hearts*, not a dualistic world.
In ordinary homes, moms bake brownies and they leave notes.
Only someone with more than a couple of years of philosophy classes could create a problem out of this.

One last comment on why it is important for us to keep a place for natural law—albeit a natural law that is in no way detached or divorced from the holy Scriptures. Natural law contextualizes the Scriptures. "Eat the brownies" makes sense only when there are brownies to eat. Without natural revelation, special revelation is nonsensical.

But more importantly, natural law contextualizes what the Scriptures are referring to when they speak of God as the Maker of Heaven and earth. He created the whole show. We live in a time when there is a great deal of postmodern pressure to push our special revelation back into the ghetto of our "faith community," or, taking it more expansively, our "faith tradition." But natural law, by definition, involves the whole house, and not just the note on the fridge—which the boys could be pressured into stuffing into the shirt pocket of their faith community.

Special revelation is the specific revelation left to us by the One who created Heaven and earth—the ultimate metanarrative. Both forms of revelation are metanarratives, and apart from the other, neither one is.

At the same time, it is easier for the unbeliever to say that "you Christians have your Bible, and the Muslims have the Koran," and so on, than it is for them to say "you Christians have your universe, and the Muslims have theirs." They *try* to make this last statement, some of them, but the laughter of the crowd is discouraging.

No, the universe is what it is, and that is the spoken word of Jesus. There is of course no place to stand outside the authority of Scripture, but this fact is easier to ignore than the fact that there is no place to stand outside the way reality is. Reality is not optional, and it is necessary for Christians to say that the authoritative law spoken by that reality is not optional either. And if there is any carping left, all we need to do at that stage is point to the note on the fridge.

## SECULAR?

There are two kinds of secularism. Well, at least two—or at least two that I am willing to write about now.

We are more accustomed to one of these, the one that refers to the functional godlessness of our public affairs. The secular state is for us that which has enshrined agnosticism as the official faith of the nation and which fights off every attempt to ground our public affairs in any transcendent realities. Not only is this infidelity, it is also incoherent.

But there is another use of the word *secular*. In the Roman Catholic communion, the secular clergy are those who (as opposed to the regular clergy) have not taken monastic vows. They live out in the world (*saeculum*), pumping their own gas and stuff. Regular clergy place themselves under a monastic rule (*regulum*) and take vows of chastity, poverty, and obedience. But obviously, the distinction here is not between those clergy who believe in God and those who do not. The distinction has to do with what is dedicated to God in this way as opposed to that which is dedicated to God in another way. I am not here defending Roman monasticism, obviously, but am simply talking about what the word *secular* can mean. It need not mean godless agnosticism. That is not the history of the word.

And so if we were to reason by analogy, this use of the word *secular* to describe our civil affairs is fully appropriate. The secular world is the non*ecclesiastical* world. But you don't have to be in church to believe in God and trust in Christ. A man who is a minister holds ecclesiastical office. A man who is an alderman or a senator holds a secular office. Should the secular world acknowledge who Jesus is? Well, of course. We don't believe that all Christians need to be ministers. But we do believe that all people should be Christians.

There is a certain sense in which a fully sanctified world will still be profane. The worship of God proper, the *cultus*, occurs at the center, in the Holy of Holies, and in turn affects everything else. When we say that *cultus* drives culture, we do not mean to say that *cultus* makes digital copies of itself, spreading through all the world until eventually all the meetings of the water sewer districts in the world are conducted like high level seminary classes. The Great Commission does not turn the world into a perpetual quiet time, where everyone walks around with that holy glow.

I put a distinction between the Church and the Kingdom. The Church is at the center, Word and sacrament, and only sacred things are sacred. Because what the Church does is potent, this transforms the entire world—but it doesn't turn the world into Church. *That's not the transformation.* The Church turns the world into what the world ought to be. The Church doesn't bring auto mechanics into the sanctuary. The Church teaches in such a way that auto mechanics grows and matures into what auto mechanics really should be like.

There will always be a center; in this sense there will always be a temple. And there will always be sanctified things (not sanctifying things) outside that temple, in front of it—*pro fanum*, before the temple.

The Church is formal worship, the *cultus*. The Kingdom is the culture that surrounds the Church, having grown out of it. The reformational work of reclaiming education or the fine arts is Kingdom work, done by Christians, to be distinguished from the formal work of the Church, done by ministers, elders, deacons, and congregants. The "task" of the Church is Word and sacrament, period. Other tasks taken up by the Church should be auxiliary works, subordinate to those central tasks, and directly related to them (e.g., building a facility in which to preach the Word and administer the sacraments, and trying diligently to keep that building from looking like your local Costco warehouse).

Rightly established, the Church equips the saints for works of service, and these works include all the things that men and women are lawfully called to do—merchandizing and mining, poetry and police work, and education and eggplant farming. The Church's task is to equip and inspire—not to supplant. When this understanding gets gummed up, then an ecclesiocentric vision goes bad, and metastasizes into one where the Church becomes the only real thing that matters. Rich nobles start leaving all their holdings to monasteries so that monks with their heads bobbing might pray for the soul of Sir Herbert Leslie Throckmorton for the next five hundred years. That's not good. The nucleus is not the cell, and the Church is not the Kingdom. The Church is not supposed to be the Death Star.

So I don't want the Church to be everything, and I don't want the reformation of the Church to be the only item on the agenda—just the first and most important item on the agenda. When that reformation begins to take shape and numerous Christians are worshiping in the way Christians ought to be worshiping, those Christians—who happen to be politicians, auto mechanics, teachers, film directors, news anchors, poets, and cafeteria workers—will begin to live out the kind of Christian life that they learned about the previous Sunday. *That* will effect the transformation of society, but not by turning that society into a giant worship service.

## IS CHRISTENDOM CONSERVATIVE, LIBERAL, BOTH, OR NEITHER?

At the beginning of his *Republocrat*, Carl Trueman says quite rightly that "religious conservatism does not demand unconditional political conservatism."[135]

The word *conserve* is a transitive verb, and there is no virtue or vice in any transitive verb. So you love, but what do you love? God? Ice cream? Child porn? The church you were baptized in? Your favorite pair of jeans? So you conserve, but what is it you want to conserve? The Kremlin Old

---

135   Carl Trueman, *Republocrat: Confessions of a Liberal Conservative* (Phillipsburg, NJ: Presbyterian & Reformed, 2010) xvii.

Guard? Redwoods? Your stock options? The legacy of the
first Christendom?

Same with *progress*. You want to progress? Great. Where?
To what end? By what standard?

Trueman's book begins with the premise that whatever political critter we wind up being, it will be some genetically
engineered combination of a donkey and an elephant. The
politics of us in the kingdom must arise from some combination of the options offered to us by the worldlings.

I, along with Trueman, do want to offer a mash-up of political options. But what I want to combine is the accomplish-
ments of the Holy Spirit thus far in the growth of Christendom, maintaining what is still here and recovering that which
once was here and needs to be brought back. In that sense, I
am conservative.

In another sense, I am progressive, wanting to move forward to all the political blessings set forth by the prophet
Isaiah. I don't want a chicken in every pot, but rather a feast of
fat things on the mountain of the Lord, a feast of wine on the
lees, and of fat things full of marrow (Is. 25:6). In that sense,
and only in that sense, I am a progressive.

If Jesus didn't do it through His Spirit, it is not worth conserving, and if Jesus isn't working toward that end by means
of His Spirit, it isn't worth working toward, either.

So this is a conservatism calculated to biff on the side of
the head the most airbrushed Republican talking point out
there, mess up his hair, and get him completely off message. This is a potent and virulent conservatism. And it is a

progressivism that actually has a scriptural definition of what might constitute *progress*, and hence is the sort of thing to make your average progressive radical go white in the face. He starts yelling about theocracy not because he is opposed to theocracy, but rather because he wanted the state to be that god, and not Jesus. A bit of tough luck for him, because the state wasn't crucified and didn't come back from the dead on the third day.

What about the third way, the way of libertarianism? Hard libertarianism or anarchy is a function of what might be called civic fatherlessness. Just as the antitheist regards the eternality of the Father as tyrannical on the face of it, so also the hard libertarian regards any civic authority whatever as something to chafe the soul.

Within this paradigm, all political authority is based on coercion, straight up, and since coercion is (obviously) bad, then at best we should regard political authority as a necessary evil, and at worst a tyranny to be thrown off. Those who are more eschatologically minded long for the day when the state withers, or blows up, or something, and then every man can sit fatherless under his own fig tree. This view assumes that the only possible justification for civil authority is pragmatic, and when we grow past the need for such pragmatic expedients, then we will no longer have any presidents or kings. We will have grown out of our need for civil fathers, or so the pipe dream goes.

But although I am in my sixties, and my father is in his eighties, he is still very much an authority in my life, and the respect I owe to him is truly significant. But suppose I were telling this to a libertarian friend, and he said that it was just because I was afraid of a spanking. That would obviously be ridiculous, even though there is a grain of truth there—that arrived about five decades late. Godly fathers do establish their authority by love and discipline, but the house they are building is not the same as the scaffolding. When a son grows to maturity, the scaffolding comes down and the fatherly authority remains. We do not grow *out of* our need for discipline by our authorities without growing *into* something else. And what we grow into is not a vacuum above us.

Scripture tells little children that their honor of their father and mother is rendered through obedience (Eph. 6:1). When children are grown, the honor is still required, but it is rendered through different means. When the children are grown, they are supposed to honor father and mother through financial support (Mark 7:11–12). The surrounding duties are different because the central duty is the same.

In an analogous way, an unruly and ungodly people must be ruled in a rough and tumble fashion (1 Tim. 1:9). But as their capacity for self-government grows (which is possible only through the gospel), they discover that, in their maturity, they can see things about their rulers that were not clear to them before. "And the Lord made Solomon very great in the sight of all Israel and bestowed on him such royal majesty as had not been on any king before him in Israel" (1 Chr. 29:25). "The God of Israel has spoken; the Rock of Israel has said to me: When one rules justly over men, ruling in the fear of

God, he dawns on them like the morning light, like the sun shining forth on a cloudless morning, like rain that makes grass to sprout from the earth" (2 Sam. 23:4).

And of course, in our day, when we really are dealing with various tyrannies that do not have the fear of God as a political consideration at all, the key phrase to focus on in the previous passage is "when one rules justly over men, ruling in the fear of God." What we have now is a ganglion of thieves "ruling impudently over men, ruling in the arrogance of man." But even so, we still salute the office.

## ESTABLISHED CHURCH?

The advocate of mere Christendom, in which role I have been placing myself, must at some point address the question of whether or not we should have an established church. And, if so, which one? We already asked the Holy Ghost Lightning Tabernacle, but they declined.

There are layers to this, making it a fun activity, like eating a birthday cake. There are constitutional issues, wisdom issues, historical issues, and scriptural issues, at least, and so let us treat them in that order.

When the Constitution of the United States was adopted, the First Amendment addressed the issue of an established church at the *federal* level, but this did not address the Christendom question. It has been made to address it by means of revisionist history, but originally it had nothing whatever to do with it. The Constitution forbade a Church of the United States on *federal* grounds, not on *secular* grounds. The document was dated in the year of our *Lord* 1789, and at the time it was adopted, nine out of the thirteen states had established churches on the state level. There was no sense in which the nonestablishment clause was violated by those states having official state religions.

Now this does not make establishment at the state level a good idea. It simply makes it a valid *constitutional* option. Patrick Henry, who grew up in Presbyterian and Anglican circles, was appalled by the flogging of a Baptist preacher under the laws of Virginia, as would I have been. That kind of thing should repulse us all.

If various states have their state birds and state flowers, there is no problem if the national government adopts the bald eagle, and whatever flower it was they adopted. But if the state establishment is Congregational in Connecticut and Episcopalian at the national level, you are just asking for trouble. Since the Founders weren't asking for trouble, and were creating a *federal* government (which is distinct from a *national* government), they removed from Congress the authority to create a national church. And good for them.

After the War Between the States, the Fourteenth Amendment was adopted, and, sometime later, court decisions retroactively applied the restrictions of the earlier amendments to the states—with the central government as the arbiter. This was a reversal of the form of government established by the Founders (as a glance at the Tenth Amendment should reveal), where the states jealously guarded what the central government could and could not do.

So if we are going by original intent, there is nothing un-constitutional about (say) South Dakota establishing the Lu-theran Church as its official denomination. Would that be a good idea? In the abstract, I don't think so, but it would be preferable to what we have now.

What are the wisdom issues? A strong argument can be made that establishment (official recognition and tax sup-port for the churches) is the spiritual kiss of death for those churches. As a general rule, we do not look for spiritual vi-brancy among all the state's kept clerics. This is kind of obvi-ous, and, in fact, the obviousness of it has been used by many to argue for the (completely unrelated) point that the civil government does not need to conduct its business in the light of Christ's lordship. But tax support for churches and recog-nition that Jesus outranks the highest human authority are distinct questions. Thus it is possible for someone (myself, for instance) to argue *against* establishment and *in favor of* our forms of government being explicitly Christian. I would want a federal republican system among civil entities, all of which are explicitly and formally Christian, and some of which may have formal church establishments. Speaking postmillenni-ally, I would want those establishments to be gradually set aside, but having them isn't the end of the world, either.

Historically, things get even more interesting. As men-tioned in chapter two, there are three basic options when it comes to Church/state relations. You can have the Church in charge of the state, as it was with the medieval settlement; you can have the state in charge of the Church, as in Erastianism;

and you can have the Church and state occupying their respective spheres of authority—with each sphere established
directly by God and neither one having to answer to the other
for its basic marching orders. During the Reformation, you
had varying degrees of balance between the second and third
options. There were certainly elements of Erastianism (the
Westminster Assembly was convened by Parliament, for example, and answered to Parliament), and the Reformers expected the civil magistrate to suppress blasphemies, and so
on. At the same time, there were battles in which, for example, Calvin resisted the right of the city council to tell him
that he couldn't excommunicate the Libertines. Discerning
the boundary between spheres of authority was easier said
than done, but both the Reformers and the civil magistrates
agreed that there *was* a boundary there that needed to be
patrolled.

As noted, the American form of the Westminster Confession redrew that boundary, not requiring establishment, but
requiring that the state recognize and protect "the church of
our common Lord."

The fact that the American revisers urged us to see that
Baptists, Presbyterians, Congregationalists, and Episcopa-
lians all served a common Lord, and were entitled to civil protections *in that capacity*, is quite striking. But the fact
that many of their heirs and assigns have thrown this into
an ecclesiastical blender, and argue that this means the civil
government must be blind to the differences between Buddhists, Muslims, Jews, Christians, atheists, and Estonian feet

fetishers tells us something equally striking, but not quite so edifying. Nothing is plainer than that a radical two-kingdom approach to Church and state is out of conformity with the American form of the Westminster Confession.

The scriptural point is this. The magistrate has a responsibility to recognize that Jesus rose from the dead and that He is seated at the right hand of God, the Father Almighty, Maker of heaven and earth. This is a scriptural requirement because the Bible says that *every* tongue must confess this. He has a responsibility to govern the nation with that truth in his mind and heart and to consult with the Church when he has questions about what it all means. He should also have the authority to tell the Church to pipe down when clerics who don't understand economics wax indignant about coffee bean plantations, as they like to do sometimes. He should propose an amendment to the Constitution that consists of the text of the Apostles' Creed. He should not put any particular denomination on the dole. If we don't like welfare queens, we should not want to encourage bishop queens. We have enough of those already.

There are three institutions among men that were created directly by God. These three institutions do not depend for their existence or authority on the good pleasure of either of the other two. These three spheres each stand alone before God, and so they are called by God to learn how to stand together, in harmony, under the common lordship of Christ. These three governments are family government (Gen. 2:22–25), civil government (Rom. 13:1), and Church government

(Eph. 4:10–12). We have the authority under Christ to create other, lesser spheres, but these are the three from God. Our task is to balance them rightly, not add to them, or subtract from them.

## SHOULD WE LET THEM IMMANENTIZE THE ESCHATON?

Two great Christian heresies—Marxism and Islam—borrowed something from the Christian faith which Christians should ask to have returned. They borrowed it and used it to great effect, and Christians, for some reason, allowed them to, neglecting it ourselves. That "thing" they borrowed was a sense of inevitable victory for their cause. But they do not have the promises of such victory, and we do. Mainland China and Saudi Arabia will be as full of the knowledge of the Lord as the waters cover the sea. Marxists sustained themselves by means of a blind faith in the inexorable forces of dialectical materialism. Islam has always depended upon conquest, and so they have never been quite the same since Lepanto and Malta.

All the nations of the earth will stream to Christ. It is unbelief to place the fulfillment outside the course of history, to hold that the promises to the nations will only come to fruition when the nations are no more.

Now the revolutionary thinks that his inevitability is within reach. We never see revolutionaries with their agitprop crowds, protesting for the cameras thusly: "What do we want!" "Peace!" (or "Whatever!") "When do we want it?" "In the eschaton!" Revolution is necessarily impatient. One exception, more or less, will be noted later.

The person who locates all transformation outside time and history really has learned how to use the Christian faith within the boundaries contained by Marx's taunt—as the opiate of the masses. By and by, in the sky, when we die, good things will happen. We gave it a big name to console ourselves, mixed in a little already but not yet, and, *blam*, we were good to go. In this instance, "going" means "sitting here, and maybe taking some seminary classes."

But Reformation faith takes note of Christopher Dawson's wonderful observation—the Christian Church lives in the light of eternity and can afford to be patient. In patience we are to possess our souls. And we can know that our labor in the Lord is not in vain (1 Cor. 15:58) because there is a direct line of continuity between what we (each of us) do right now, and the conversion of the nations.

What I am trying to do is persuade Christians that we will win the race and that we should run it as those who intend to win it. I am not trying to persuade them that the race is a brief little burst, a 100-yard dash. No, it is a couple marathons, end to end, and we have barely started. But we are running to win, and not to place or show.

So what should we want now? We should want Christians to *know* this now—they don't have to *do* it all now. The martyrs who went to their deaths in the first century were building the Christendom that did not begin to appear for several centuries after that. *Patience.*

When it comes to our secular arrangements, I am not trying to get Christians to vote it out in the next election cycle. That's not going to happen, and fine. What *can* happen, and what is happening, is a large number of people realizing that secularism is the joke that fell flat. This too shall pass.

One revolutionary, the exception mentioned earlier, who did have a longer view than did Lenin was named Gramsci. He advocated a strategy for the West that has proven—from the perspective of the revolutionaries—far more potent than Lenin's impatient violence. He urged what he called "the long march through the institutions." Lenin's approach was taken in the East, and Gramsci's in the West. Lenin did an enormous amount of damage, but Gramsci did more. Like the violent revolutionaries, this slow approach cultivates a sense of inevitability.

That sense of inevitability is potent, even with false faiths, if only for a time. How much more potent will it be when Christians understand that the gospel is all about world conquest and when they will be content with nothing less than world conquest? I know that place where I labor—the Pacific Northwest—will one day be overwhelmingly Christian. This will happen long after I am dead, and long before Jesus returns. This is reformational transformation, not revolutionary zeal.

This "conquest" will be accomplished by means of God's weakness, not man's strength, for our weapons are not carnal. This thing will be done—and it will be done—in the power of the Spirit by means of words and water, bread and wine.

What are we doing? We are besieging strongholds, and the citadels of unbelief will fall. Every sermon is another swing of the battering ram, every baptism is an engine deployed to overthrow the devil, and every administration of the Supper is an inexorable offer of wine for the forgiveness of the world and bread for the life of the world. And the day is coming, when they will receive it.

Since the very beginning, the Christian faith has had to deal with imposters who gain control of the governmental mechanisms of the Church, doing so in order to undermine the entire point of the Church. Think, for example, of Diotrephes, who would put out of the Church anybody who had even voted in favor of receiving emissaries of the apostles (3 John 9–10). That man had control of the perks of preeminence; he had control of the minutes and file cabinets; he had control of the office keys. The only thing He didn't have control of was the Spirit. The Spirit blows where He wills.

The intention, laid out for us in Scripture, is for the institutional Church to receive the apostles, their emissaries, and their letters. When we get their letters, we in the Church are supposed to open them up *and do what they say.* Unfortunately, Diotrephes has an online discipleship training program, and his imitators are everywhere. Moreover, his imitators and heirs are, just like he was, entrenched in the Church.

But this should not be a surprise. We are also taught in Scripture that the process of getting from our raggety-taggety beginnings to the point where the bride walks down the aisle without spot or any other blemish is supposed to be a long and arduous process. That process is called Church history, and it is what we might call the mother of all extreme makeovers. It is not a sign that God's purposes have been successfully thwarted; it is the way He determined to accomplish them. When we grapple with the issues that this creates (and it creates a ton of them), we are simply doing our lessons.

During periods of reformation and revival, the Church really is quickened. She grows and spreads and flourishes. Now if culture is religion externalized, as Henry Van Til noted, it is not long before these lively forms of the faith take on an external cultural manifestation. But what happens when the liveliness dies away (as it frequently does), and the forms remain? We have those who love the forms of religion, but who deny the power of it (2 Tim. 3:5). We have heirs of Chrysostom who mutter their way through prayer books. We have heirs of Ursinus who doodle in the margins of their book of discipline, trying to make it into a confessional Book of Kells with their colored sharpies. No gospel sense of righteousness any more, but *real* pretty.

Another way of thinking about this is that the Holy Spirit's fire is the kind of fire that forms and builds its own altars, those altars it comes to rest upon. But what happens when the fire goes out a generation or two later, and the altar is still there? The natural response is to try to fix things by decorating the altar, bringing in embellishments and bronze gewgaws galore. But without the fire, a decorated altar is still a cold one.

Every form of Christendom thus far has been a visible, civic result of a potent visible Church. And a potent visible

Church has always been the result of a vibrant movement of the Holy Spirit, bringing the new birth to countless individuals. This new birth is invisible; you can see its effects, but you cannot watch it directly. The fire in the illustration above is the new birth, and there is no other fire.

When the new birth is there, the valley of dry bones becomes the mustering point for a great army. When the new birth is not there, all the arranging and planning and fussing that we might be able to do will not accomplish anything. Ezekiel was told to *preach* to the bones, not to line up all the femurs in a tidy confessional row. As Lloyd-Jones said about some ecumenical endeavor or other, "Putting all the ecclesiastical corpses into one graveyard will not bring about a resurrection."

Christendom, by definition, has to do with physical, public embodiment. It is public and external. It can be photographed. But if American Christians succeeded in having the Apostles' Creed put into our Constitution, we would not thereby have a new nation in the new Christendom. We would have something like England, a teetery relic nation from the old Christendom. England is a Christian nation on *paper*. We cannot fix our problems on paper, or with paper. What we need is fire.

And we cannot have fire without preachers of the gospel who know what they are about. We need preachers who have experienced the new birth themselves and who know what the Bible teaches about the necessity of it. And we need preachers who have experienced the anointing of the Holy

Spirit on their pulpit declarations, who know what real power is. Further, we need more than one of them. Two or three thousand should do it.

We should not have to choose between the fire and the altar. We want both. We want a reformation and revival in the Church, and we want a renewed Church that then does not shrink back from its appointed role in establishing an institutional altar to burn hot on. But in wanting both, at this point in history, we want the fire first. Who wants a collection of cold altars? When the fire falls (as it will), we will shortly have altars enough.

## HOW DO WE DISTINGUISH PRINCIPLES AND PLOT POINTS?

One of the first things to distinguish is someone who wants to go the same place you do, but has a different view about how best to do it, from someone who wants to go somewhere completely different, but wants to use the same methods you are using. Distinguish principles and methods—where you are going is more important than how you get there. This is not to say that how you get there is unimportant; it is simply less important.

So if one man wants to drive to the East Coast in a Ford, he has more in common with a man who wants to do the same thing in a Chevy than he does with another man driving to the West Coast in a Ford. Couple this with the fact that it is possible to pass someone on the road who is going the opposite direction, and at the precise moment when you do that, you are in exactly the same spot. Further, somebody else who is going to the *same* place you are might be a hundred miles behind you.

And sometimes it is hard to tell, when you are in the same spot, if you actually are headed in opposite directions. The whole thing can be quite confusing. All of Israel thought that Reuben and Gad were veering off into idolatry when they weren't (Josh. 22:15–16), and Paul saw and understood that Peter was fatally compromising the gospel when it came to seating arrangements at the Antioch potluck though it almost certainly would not have occurred to Peter to put it like that (Gal. 2:11). Barnabas saw that Paul was headed in the right direction before anybody else saw that (Acts 9:27), and Paul saw that Peter was headed in a wrong direction before anybody else saw *that*.

Changing the subject only slightly, my mother went to Prairie Bible Institute back in the day, an institution that at the time, was using temporary buildings. Why not nice stone and brick buildings? Well, the president said, he had no interest in building nice buildings for the liberals. Since everything always goes liberal, let's keep what we build for them at a minimum. Now it is easy to laugh at this, but did anything happen in the twentieth century to actually put the lie to this pessimistic assumption?

The policy is shortsighted, *if* it is shortsighted, because it doesn't line up with Scripture, and not because experience has taught us that evangelical seminaries, publishing houses, denominations, and colleges never go liberal. I believe that

things are getting better over the long haul because of the
prophet Isaiah and the Psalms of David, and *not* because
*Christianity Today*, InterVarsity Press, and the Presbyterian
Church in America have inspired me by a rock-ribbed bibli-
cism that grows stauncher by the year.

Now in *this* context, what statement is being made when
you team up with somebody? A lot depends on the nature of
the yoke. If you are ordaining someone to the local session,
you ought to be saying that you believe there is a fundamental like-mindedness. If you invite someone to speak at your
conference, it means, at the least, that you want to be friends
and that you believe his ministry is going more good than
harm. Or maybe it is doing more harm than good, but not
by much, and you want to play the role of Priscilla and Aq-
uila to his Apollos (Acts 18:26) simply because the *trajectory*
is promising.

You play cards with the hand you are dealt. You don't stare
at a lousy hand, and resolve the problem by wishing upon a
star. That's not a move found in Hoyle.

In order to sort all this out, you have to have a sharp and
clear distinction between the fundamentals and the second-
aries, and you have to have the right kind of suspicious mind
concerning your own rascal heart. Rascal hearts find the
wrong thing to do at the wrong time just as sure as raccoons
find the garbage cans. Someone who is sound on the fundamentals, but who has a quirk or two and more personality
than you might like is a prime candidate for you to set up a
hue and cry against. His talent makes him a threat to your

esteemed position, and his quirks make him vulnerable to the charge that he is not the kind of confessional man we want to encourage. Turf wars in the body of Christ have always been common enough, but they still need to be decked out in the appropriate vocabulary. "Strikes at the vitals," and "compromising the gospel" are very useful phrases, or at least they are if this kind of thing appeals to you.

With this said, what issues are fundamental in our day? This is key—one of the common mistakes is that of thinking that the decisive point in the sixteenth century has to be the decisive point today. This is yet another failure to read the narrative right. Principles are constant, *but plot points aren't.* But, lest this point be mistaken, as it always is, our Protestant fathers in the sixteenth century were right to take the stand they did, and the pope and his council were wrong.

However, the fact that I cheer for one side over the other at the battle of Gettysburg does not mean the battle of Gettysburg is still being fought. We are at a different place in the war; the terrain is different and the circumstances are different. The uniforms are different, but the long war is always the same.

Surrendering a place that is *currently* being contested, and justifying this surrender because you are a sound military historian and understand who was in the right at Gettysburg, is folly and cowardice. Attacking others in your army who are courageously fighting where the current battle is raging, and all because you suspect that they are not as sound as they could be on Gettysburg, is more folly and more cowardice.

But before moving on, let me affirm, once more, three ba-
sics. I embrace the five *solas*, I whoop until hoarse for the
five points of Calvinism, and I heartily lament Jeb Stuart's
ill-fated ride around the battle.

Where is the battle now? What are the issues that threaten
the purity of the gospel now? Where are the compromises
*now*?

The real rot that *we* must contend with begins with Darwin, not Bonaventure, and any and all accommodations with
Darwin. Darwin gave modernity the mechanism it needed to
throw off the authority of God's Word and the sovereignty
of the Lord Christ. Darwin is foundational to the secularist
modernity project, but there is more. He is also foundational
to the postmodern goo cauldron that is our culture today and
to every form of what I have called pomosexuality. It is striking that postmodernists never want to be post-Darwinian.
The whole thing, modernity and postmodernity, is part of
one sustained play in the football game. Modernity was the
quarterback in the shotgun position, and postmodernity is
the quick pass to the flat. When someone helpfully tells me
that the receiver in the flat is *post*shotgun, my response will
generally be to tell them that I don't find their distinctions all
that helpful.

And this is why theistic evolution is a big deal, and this is
why compromises with every form of gender-bending is a big
deal. And this is also why a large number of people who are
"contending for the gospel" . . . aren't really.

# WHAT IS THE DIFFERENCE BETWEEN ALLIES AND COBELLIGERENTS?

Should Christians work together with secularist conservatives in pursuit of shared "common sense" goals? The answer is that I would be fully willing, sure—if the secularists get spooked at the size of the national deficit, and turn off the spigot, they can count on my support. And if the Mormons in southern Idaho got a pro-life referendum on the ballot, I would cheerfully vote for it. That part of life is simple. Allies, cobelligerents, all that. An ally fights the same enemy you are fighting, and for the same reasons. A cobelligerent fights them for different reasons.

The complicating factor is that of oaths and the rendering of unlawful allegiances as the price of admission to their game. One of the myths that has been spread about religious conservatives is that they don't know how to bend or compromise (this being the supposed source of their propensity to violence), and the corresponding myth on the other side is that secularists are calm, cool, and collected, and ever ready to make adjustments as the demands of the present reality dictate.

But our secularists are actually hard-line sectarians. They will brook no compromise on *these* issues. We do not have a parliamentary system where a secularist party can form a coalition with ultraconservatives with funny hats. We have a winner-take-all system, and the absolute demand that secularists place on religious conservatives is avowed allegiance to the secularist arrangement. They make us take these oaths so many times and in so many ways that we scarcely notice them anymore.

Say that a controversy arises over a cross in a county seal or a Christmas tree on the town courthouse steps. The conservative secularists will bend far enough to say that the cross or tree should be allowed to stay, just so long as everybody involved in the support of such symbols *promises that they don't mean anything by it.* If there were any indication that these religious symbols were being taken seriously, the whole coalition would blow apart. They will allow us certain things for the sake of our nostalgia, but nothing of real importance and not for any more substantive reason. As we move to their secularist paradise across the ocean, they will allow us to take a few trinkets to remember the old country by, and they do this because they know those trinkets are going to wind up in a shoebox in the attic.

All I am saying is that while I am willing to work with them, I will not do so on their terms, and I won't take any of their oaths. Jesus is Lord, and I want Him to be acknowledged as such everywhere and by everybody. They have no response to this other than to accuse me of being an extreme member of Reformed Taliban, eager to start setting IEDs by the side of Highway 95. These guys are a hoot. But I am a Burkean conservative, and I don't want to achieve any of my sociopolitical goals by revolutionary means. Earlier I cited Christopher Dawson's maxim that the Christian Church lives in the light of eternity and can afford to be patient. But the Church also lives in the light of the holiness of God and cannot afford to be dishonest.

The issue cannot be avoided, because every time a relevant controversy arises, the accusations of Church and state relations arise. If some secularist politico sap forgets himself, and prays at some event in Jesus' name, the cry goes up, "Constantinianism! How dare he!" All I am saying is that such a moment is supposed to be our cue to rush in there, saying, *no, no, nothing of the kind*, and that we should simply refuse to take our cue. See what happens. I can assure you that lots of interesting things will happen.

## BUT ISN'T POLITICS DIRTY?

James Davison Hunter has this to say about contemporary Christian political involvement: "These qualifications notwithstanding, the reality is that politics is the tactic of choice for many Christians as they think about changing the world . . . . It is not an exaggeration to say that *the dominant public witness of the Christian churches in America since the early 1980s has been a political witness.*" [136]

Yeah, but. An important qualification has to be added to this. Before offering that addition, however, let me say that I acknowledge that there *are* evangelical Christians out there who are political wonks and junkies in a way that is not spiritually healthy. That said (in order to demonstrate that I am as evenhanded and as balanced as can be), let me proceed to add my qualification.

Think about this for a moment. The "most dominant public witness" of Christians has been political. Assuming this is

136  Hunter, 12.

accurate (and I believe it is), there are different reasons why it
might be so. One reason could be that Christians are the ones
with the problem. They have politics on the brain. They rush
to the mechanisms of the state (which were modestly hiding
in a distant village), in order to advance their public faith with
the politics of coercion. In other words, these Christians have
lost faith in Jesus their Savior, and are trying to use the political process as a sort of savior's-little-helper.

Another option, and one that I consider far more likely, is
this. The political state in our day is swollen and overgrown
and has gotten into everything. Politics, the great secular idol
of modernity, has virtually filled up every public space. This
means that it is not possible to go into any public space in
order to have a public witness of any kind without it resulting
in some kind of political confrontation.

To this extent, blaming public Christians for being "too
political" is like blaming Noah's ark for being "too wet."

Abortion and sodomy were sins long before they were
constitutional rights. If a minister preached against them a
thousand years ago, he was preaching against moral failings,
and he was not being political. He was being public, but not
political. When I do it, I am preaching against moral failings,
too, but I am also being political. What changed? It wasn't the
Decalogue. It wasn't the history of the Church or the history
of preaching. It wasn't the nature of the gospel. It wasn't *me*.
Rather, it was the nature of the idol being challenged—and
this idol aspires to omnipresence.

We are told, *ad nauseam*, to keep our morality out of politics. It would be more to the point to tell the idolmongers to keep their politics out of morality. Public morality need not be political in the sense we are discussing. Public morality need not be a matter that concerns the legislature. But if the legislature concerns itself with everything, then any faithful Christian expression will immediately be concerned with the political.

The secular polis is an in-your-face polis. The polis tells me what kind of light bulbs I must have, how far apart my sheetrock screws have to be, whether or not I can smoke in a restaurant that wants to let me, whether or not I can remove that tag from my mattress, and whether I can say that sodomy is a sin from the pulpit, whether or not it is in my text. In short, if I step into any public space in the name of Jesus Christ, I will be indignantly told, almost immediately, that this space is taken, and not to be a claim-jumper. I may (for the present) believe in Jesus behind my eyes and between my ears, but if it goes any further than that, I am clearly out of control. I am meddling with politics.

In his essay on membership in *The Weight of Glory*, C.S. Lewis says this: "in the first place, when the modern world says to us aloud, 'You may be religious when you are alone,' it adds under its breath, 'and I will see to it that you are never alone.'"[137] This is the kind of thing we are up against.

Our task as Christians is therefore not to jump on the back of this monster politics, in order to tame it so that it does what

137   C.S. Lewis, *The Weight of Glory* (New York: HarperOne, 2001), 160.

we want instead of what our opponents want. Politics, in its current manifestation, is a fire-breathing dragon—and we are called to play the part of St. George and kill this thing. And what would St. George say if he were upbraided for being too focused on the dragon, for being too interested in the dragon issues of the day? He could say, if he had his wits about him, that he was only going to be focused on the dragon issues until it was dead—which should be another hour or so.

Darryl Hart provides a good overview of recent interactions of the state and evangelicals and the attempt to have the government provide help to various "faith-based" social agencies. He does good work pointing out the corners that we have painted ourselves into, but his narrow conception of what the Church is called to do means that his critique is not as pointed as it could have been.

> The all-or-nothing logic inherent in appeals to the Lordship of Christ also fails to do justice to the reduced character of Christ's sovereignty in the Christian era . . . . The problem with blurring the claims of the Old and New Testaments is that Christ's kingdom in the latter was fundamentally different from the kingdom of Israel in the former. The kingdom of Christ was a spiritual entity, not a political one, and it had every appearance during the church's early history of coexisting with non-Christian empires.[138]

---

138  Hart, 230.

But the Church coexisted in the early centuries with pagan empires only in the same way that the United States coexisted with Nazi Germany and Imperial Japan in 1942.

Hart is confusing the relationship of the Church to mercy ministries generally, and the relationship of the Church to tax-driven "mercy" ministries. The former is of course required of us by James—true religion is to keep our ourselves unstained by the world and to visit widows and orphans in their affliction. The spirituality of the Church cannot be construed to mean that we are allowed to limit ourselves to visiting spiritual widows and ethereal orphans. The latter has a lot in common with the view held by Judas—he was concerned that the money spent by the woman with the ointment hadn't been given to the poor in the approved way, which is to say, the way in which he could skim a piece of the action.

"In other words," Hart continues, "by pitting a religious-friendly state as the opposite of a secular government, the Lordship of Christ outlook fails to do justice to the real genius of the American founding, which was to try to take religion out of the hands of civil authorities and allow believers to practice their faith according to their own consciences."[139] But here is the difficulty. Of *course* the state does not have the right to be secular. The state does not have the right to refuse to acknowledge the claims of Jesus Christ. Of course the state does not have a special dispensation from God that

139 Ibid., 230.

allows them to be religiously agnostic any more than God would give them a dispensation to embrace any other form of unbelief.

Precisely *because* the state does not have the right to be secular, precisely *because* the state is required to honor the Lordship of Jesus Christ, the state *may not* barge into people's homes and rob them of their hard-earned money in the name of redistributing the wealth a bit. To do so is called *stealing*. Taxing the people in order to perform a function that God did not assign to the state is called *theft*. The state does not have the right to say, "I am stealing from you . . . because, because, um . . . because of the Lordship of Jesus Christ! *That's* the ticket!" If Jezebel had taken Naboth's vineyard in the name of "social justice," or "land reform," that would not have changed the prophet's view of it. Neither would it have helped if Jim Wallis sincerely thought that Naboth was a fat cat plantation owner. Maybe he was. How does that make it somebody else's plantation now?

## TRUE CONSERVATISM

Conservative Christians ought not to be in thrall to whatever Fox News dubs to be conservative. Everything hinges on what it is you are conserving. Does conservative Christianity conserve theological truths only? Of course not—there are cultural ramifications in what we believe, e.g., the pro-life issue and the gay marriage issue. But by this I certainly do not want to say that conservative theology requires me to sign up for the Fox News brand of conservatism, the one that wants to protect the right of top-heavy starlets to fall out of their dresses, a regular event that to Fox appears constantly newsworthy. They have a theology that comes out of their halter tops.

But since real theology comes out our *fingertips*, and whatever it is that is coming out our fingertips reveals our theology, conservative theology does require some form of conservative politics and does require *some* form of a conservative cultural agenda. At the same time, because a conservative theology of Scripture will eventually result in a postmillennial eschatology (said the postmillennialist), this progressive aspect of theology will result in some form of progressive politics and some form of a progressive cultural agenda. But what we conserve and what we work to institute as progress must all be governed by Scripture. We don't get to pick and choose from the smorgasbord stocked by the lefties and righties.

So here is the central thing that we need to conserve (what we have of it), and progress toward (what we have not yet realized). We need to recognize that politics is necessarily coercive, and because coercion is a big deal, a Christian social order should want to strictly limit coercion to the bounds assigned by Scripture. Unless I have a word from God, I don't want to *make* anybody do anything.

Because of this I am willing to have tight abortion laws—I am willing to make people not kill other people. Because of this I am not willing to allow a nebulous "concern for . . . poverty"[140] to require us to throw economic realities overboard

140 Trueman, xxvii.

in a way that impoverishes a bunch of people. The man who considers the poor is blessed (Ps. 41:1), and the word for *considers* there means a practical, applied wisdom of the kind that has studied real economics, and not that impulsive sentimentalism that wrecks livelihoods in the name of Jesus. In conserving free markets, we are preserving yesterday's progress and are making more progress possible. But all of it, whether we are protecting or establishing, must be grounded in the lordship of Jesus Christ and on His revealed Word.

# 9

# SOME TOUGHER CHRISTENDOM QUESTIONS

## BIG VISION, SMALL GOVERNMENT?

The basic question in politics is this: what is our warrant for *making* people do things? George Washington once noted that government rests upon force. In the last analysis, however you want to describe it, government makes some people do what they don't want to do. The point of traction in government is therefore the point of coercion.

The fact that most people like the public arrangement and don't need to be coerced doesn't alter this basic fact. The coercion falls on the outliers, true enough, and when the force of coercion begins to fall on everyone, that is a prime indicator that the particular government concerned is not long for the world. Nevertheless, the fact that only some people are coerced doesn't make the arrangement "not coercive." Most of the tire isn't touching the road. When a lot of the tire is touching the road you have what is called a flat, and the car won't go.

So if coercion is inescapable, we should ask some tough questions about it. What is our warrant for coercing people? Who should coerced, and in what areas? What should happen to a man if he fights our attempts to make him do something?

My political philosophy is pretty simple. We should want to keep coercion to a true minimum, and we should want to have ample warrant from God Almighty for whatever coercion we impose. And if we follow the latter principle wisely, the former should take care of itself.

I want the coercive power of the state to fall on thugs and rapists, and not upon the wrong kind of light bulb user. I want force to be applied to the man who would rob a merchant of his earnings, and not applied to the merchant himself so that the government might rob him of his earnings. I want to restrict the thief with a Saturday night special, and this means I should also want to restrict the thief who does what he does with fountain pens in signing ceremonies. In short, I want coercion to fall on the wicked, and not on the righteous. "Shall the throne of iniquity have fellowship with thee, which frameth mischief by a law? They gather themselves together against the soul of the righteous, and condemn the innocent blood" (Ps. 94:20–21). "Take away the wicked from before the king, and his throne shall be established in righteousness" (Prov. 25:5).

I want the warrant for the use of force to come from Scripture. I don't want it to come out of the frenetic vaporings of global warming screechers or any other form of officious leftist meddling.

Now some worry about a tight theocratic state run by scowling exegetes whose shoes are two sizes too small, and they have asked where this leaves citizens whose activities would be proscribed by biblical law—like enthusiasts for sodomy or sharia. Those who worry about this possible problem envision a dark and dystopic Amerika when, on these two topics, it would actually look more like America in 1960. Was America in 1960 a free society? Sodomy was against the law everywhere, and no locales were carving out room for sharia.

Look. Christians believe the Bible *invented* free societies. Secularists who worry about fundamentalist Christians sneaking in to spy out their liberties are like a prodigal son buying drinks for the house while secretly worrying that his father will break into his room that night in order to steal all his money.

## TAXATION AND THEFT?

Should we say that any taxation whatever amounts to theft? And if we think that some is, and some is not, then how to tell the difference? Is it simply done on the basis of what we think is prudent?

So there are basically three questions. The first concerns whether or not there is such a thing as taxation which is not theft. And the answer is *yes*—there is such a thing as lawful taxation (Num. 3:47; Rom. 13:7). It does exist. To maintain that all taxation is theft by definition is to take a hard libertarian–anarchist view of civil government, which is not warranted by Scripture.

The second question is whether, given the lawfulness of taxation as a general question, it is possible for a government to steal. If taxation *can* be lawful, is it possible for a government to steal? And again, the answer is *yes*. If Ahab had gotten Naboth's vineyard by means of "land reform," or "zoning adjustments," or "eminent domain," such labels would not have made it any less stealing. Or if Ahab had just applied property taxes to the vineyard (total, five thousand dollars) with the entire vineyard (worth five million) being the collateral for the tax liability, then that would have been another form of stealing.

So some taxes are simply legalized stealing. Jesus tells us that the sons are exempt from taxes, and yet He has Peter pay a tax voluntarily to prevent the giving of offense (Mt. 17:25–26). The principle that can be gathered here is that a government entity *claimed* that a tax was owed, and Jesus said that it was not *really* owed. In such a circumstance, if the government takes that amount by force, the only way we could define it would be by the word "stealing."

Take this another way. If a throne can be unrighteous in general (Prov. 25:5), then a throne can be unrighteous in the specifics. God's law provides us with the very definition of unrighteousness, and this means that governments can steal.

So the third question is how do we tell the difference? Before answering, we should note that every Christian who grants that a government *can* steal is obligated to tell us where he thinks the dividing line is. The only alternative would be to maintain that the civil government has an absolute claim on all property, and that while it might let the peons "use" some of it some of the time, this is just because it is being nice.

If you believe (as I do) that it could be possible for a man to rape his wife, then you have the obligation to be able to distinguish lawful intercourse from unlawful. No human authority is absolute. If you believe (as I do) that governments can (and do) steal, then you have to be able to state where and why you think that.

Boondoggles and redistribution of wealth are clear symptoms that something has gone wrong, just as a drunken band of pirates divvying up the booty around a bonfire on the beach is a similar indication. But the act of piracy occurred *earlier*. Waste, fraud, and abuse are also symptomatic. That is what happens when pirates spend the money. What is the heart of the thievery? Where is the point when pirates *get* the money?

I would suggest that Samuel tells us. When he is warning the people of Israel about the coming predations of a king, there are numerous aspects to that warning, but one of them has to do with taxation. Samuel says that if they take a king "like the other nations," then it is conceivable that the tax rate might actually get up to ten percent (1 Sam. 8:15–17). We are so far gone in our folly that we would give anything to get *back* to ten percent.

And so here is where I would draw the line. Ten percent is significant because that is what Almighty God claims. The tithe of God is a prerogative of God. I don't believe that it is possible for a king, or a congress, or a parliament, or a president, to claim that much or more without setting itself up as a rival to God, which is exactly what our governments have done.

So, in sum, I would be happy with an 8 percent flat tax. The government may want more than that, for governments always do. But they certainly don't *need* more than that.

## HOMOSEXUALITY AND GAY MARRIAGE?

Marriage is a political act, and not an individual choice. How you marry is a way of testifying to what city you belong. Who defines marriage? The difficulty we are having in our generation in answering this question shows how theology shapes and drives everything.

If God created the world, put one man and one woman in it, married them to each other, and established that as a pattern for the rest of human history, then marriage should be defined in accordance with that reality. If He did nothing of the kind, and we actually evolved out of the primordial goo, then *we* get to shape and define it however we would like it to go.

One other item of Christian theology has to be taken into account, and that is the reality of the fall into sin. The

Christian approach to marriage in the context of mere Christendom deals with both of these realities—the creational given of male and female, and the sinful propensity we have to hump the world. Creational sexuality and sinful sexuality are both factors.

Our laws about marriage must therefore do two things, not just one. They must honor what God has established in the first place, and they must restrain (by not honoring with the recognition of marriage) any of the other forms of sexual congress that sinful men have come up with.

When Jesus taught on divorce, He appealed to the creation pattern. "And he answered and said unto them, Have ye not read, that he which made *them* at the beginning made them male and female, And said, For this cause shall a man leave father and mother, and shall cleave to his wife: and they twain shall be one flesh? Wherefore they are no more twain, but one flesh. What therefore God hath joined together, let not man put asunder" (Mt. 19:4–6).

Reasoning by analogy from this, we can see other expressions of sexuality are excluded. A man should not be allowed to marry himself. It is not good that man should be alone (Gen. 2:18). A man should not be allowed to marry multiple wives. God said that He would make a helper suitable to him (Gen. 1:18). Bestiality is excluded. Adam did not find a helper suitable to him among the animals (Gen. 2:20). Homosexuality is excluded because God brought Adam a woman, not another man (Gen. 2:22). And divorce is excluded because God is the one who brought the man and woman together (Mt. 19:6).

But of course if none of this happened, and our ancestors climbed down out of the trees circa fifteen million years ago, then evolutionary shape-shifting is the order of the day, and there is absolutely no reason not to let people marry whomever or whatever they want.

The marriage debates are a prime illustration of why governmental neutrality on basic religious issues is an impossibility. He who says A must eventually say B, and now that we are getting to the end of this seamy chain of syllogisms, we are confronted with the demand to allow homosexuals to marry. But this is not the end of it, and this shows why it is so important to get down to first principles.

The secularists want to say that in addition to straights, we have a range of options with the fetching label of LGBTQ. Anybody who thinks that list of letters won't grow just isn't paying attention. Pederasty, bestiality, heteropolygamy, heteropolyandry, and bisexual polyoptions are all waiting in the wings.

The reason why homosexual mirage won't end the debates (and the hate crimes of those who take up the wrong side of the debate) is that these marriage "reforms" clearly have not solved the problems of the bisexuals. With our arbitrary limitation of marital status to two and only two people, we are plainly telling the bisexual that he must choose between a heterosexual marriage or a homosexual marriage, but that he can't do both. "But I am both!" he wails . . . suppose this poor little buster wants to express all of his sexual yearnings within the holy bonds of matrimony, and the clerk down at the county courthouse, just seething with hate, won't give him a license with a place on it for three signatures. And then the Muslim guy, next in line, wants one with a place for four signatures.

This is all perfectly irrational, of course, but the real problem with rational consistency lies with those Christians who want to fight this latest onslaught without resorting to Genesis and the foundational authority of God's Word (in short, without fighting for mere Christendom). What these secularists (or sexularists, that works too) are advocating is perfectly consistent with their premises and with the sexual history of the human race (a sinful sexual history). This is why Christians can't fight this on the basis of "traditional values." The sexual traditions of humanity, considered apart from God's Word, have contained way too many child brides, harems, serial polygamists, and concubines to provide us with the appropriate guidance here.

If you want a knockdown argument for mere Christendom, look no further than *Obergefell v. Hodges*.

## SLAVERY?

As everyone with an Internet connection has been loudly told by now, my very favorite subject is slavery, and I am always itching for opportunities to talk about it . . . (That was sarcasm.)

Nevertheless, the subject of slavery does provide a glorious test for those Christians who claim to have very specific boundaries past which our witness for Christ cannot go. Take, for example, this comment from Michael Horton:

Both Northern and Southern churches had reduced slavery merely to a political issue when they should have done what only churches can do: proclaim God's judgment upon the kidnapping and forced labor of fellow humans and excommunicate members who refused to repent of the practice. At the same time, church members could have exercised their moral conscience in deciding for themselves how best to abolish the institution in courts and legislatures.[141]

There are two things going on here. One is the misreading of the charter that God gave to the Church. Once you have excommunicated a man for profiting from "forced labor," what will you say to the apostle Paul when Philemon goes and tells the apostle what you did to him? Probably a moot point, since the apostle's status is all tied up in the credentials committee. *He* has been in jail one too many times, and the presbytery has needed to go through some due diligence on him for some time now.

What possible basis could you have for excommunicating a church member who was obeying the New Testament injunctions to masters and, in order to be obeying them, had to be a slave owner? Assume a Christian master of Philemon's character. He is carefully applying Paul's instructions in Ephesians 6:9, Colossians 4:1, and 1 Timothy 6:2. Is he to be disciplined? What good does it do for the Church to be limited to Word and sacrament only when we refuse to take

141  Michael Horton, *Christless Christianity: The Alternative Gospel of the American Church* (Grand Rapids, MI: Baker, 2008), 214-5.

in what that Word says, when it says what it does in unambiguous prose?

> And, ye masters, do the same things unto them, forbearing threatening: knowing that your Master also is in heaven; neither is there respect of persons with him. (Eph. 6:9)

> Masters, give unto your servants that which is just and equal; knowing that ye also have a Master in heaven. (Col. 4:1)

> And they that have believing masters, let them not despise them, because they are brethren; but rather do them service, because they are faithful and beloved, partakers of the benefit. These things teach and exhort. (1 Tim. 6:2)

Now I agree with Horton that church discipline should have been applied for kidnapping. I also agree that the slave trade was therefore a monstrous traffic, and that the Church would have been well within her rights and obligations to discipline any members who engaged in it. But good luck doing that and not having a transformative effect on culture. How is eliminating the slave trade not a form of the Christless Christianity that Horton objects to?

I'll write it one more time: If the Church is not transforming the culture around her, then the culture around her is transforming the Church.

## TOLERANCE?

There are two basic points to make about tolerance as a civic virtue. The first is logical and the second historical.

The logical point is that tolerance cannot be a free-floating virtue. This is because no virtue (or vice, either) can be found in a transitive verb. It is not a matter of *whether* you tolerate, for everyone does, but rather a matter of *what* you tolerate and why.

If we were to say that Smith tolerates X, we do not yet know if Smith is a hero or a skunk. Does he tolerate respectable dissent, responsibly offered? Child porn? Smokers in bars? Transfats in restaurants? Ethnic violence? What does he tolerate? This is what Rushdoony used to call an inescapable concept—not whether, but which. As soon as a man shows his hand, and we know what he tolerates, he is put in a position where he cannot tolerate those who refuse to tolerate what he does. A wide acceptance of the homosexual agenda, for example, means that a society has to crack down on the "homophobes." Not whether, but which.

This leads to the question of what a mere Christendom would tolerate. Every organized society excludes certain behaviors by definition and is inclusive of others. This is what it means to *be* a society. Every society has shared values, and it polices on behalf of those values. When those values are not policed, you have a condition of anarchy, or what the older civic theorists used to call "a state of nature."

This being the case, it is certainly appropriate for people to ask what a member nation of this mere Christendom would tolerate, and what it would not. That is a most reasonable question. For those who gain their information about such things from the screechings of the alarmist left, the answer will perhaps be surprising.

Christians *invented* the most open and tolerant society in the history of the world. Tolerance, as we have known it historically, is a Christian virtue. As preachers of the gospel spread throughout a society and new life comes to more and more of the population, the preconditions for an open society are being established. The more the law of God is written on hearts and minds, which is what happens under the new covenant, the less necessary it is to have standards of public decency urged upon us from billboards. There were all sorts of things that, prior to the last several generations of general deterioration, went without saying. Once that consensus is gone, you have to start calling the cops for more and more situations, and freedom starts to erode.

Now some might say in protest that they are quite certain that if evangelical Christians had their way, there would be no more acts of simulated copulation on parade floats in San Francisco, which is quite true. The observer would go on to point out that such open behavior would not fly in the totalitarian hellhole that we call North Korea, and QED. But they fail to note that such frank displays of deranged yearnings would not have flown in  the truly open and free society of 1960 America, either. All freedom necessitates restraint and, for those who have been following this, the question has to do with who is restrained and for what reason.

An important part of the *how* concerns not the identity of those restrained, but their position in that society. This will have to be discussed further in its place, but are those being restrained at the center of that society, or are they outliers? Is the standard enforced with fines ten times a day, or twice every ten years?

Free societies can function only when the authority of restraint is found in the old fashioned virtues of self-restraint and self-control. Free governments presuppose self-government. This is why John Adams said that our Constitution presupposes a moral and religious people—it is, he said, "wholly unfit for any other." And it *is* wholly unfit for any other.

All this said, it remains an ineradicable part of the historical record that free societies arose and grew out of Christian societies. I am arguing that there is a connection and that this is not mere coincidence. I am arguing for a return to the preconditions of civic freedom, and am not arguing for an abandonment of them. Unbelief does not generate free societies. Out of all the explicitly atheistic societies that formed over the course of the last century, how many of them were open and free societies? Ah . . .

For secularists to treat believing Christians as the principal threat to their freedoms would be, were it not so serious, not very serious. But that goes without saying.

So as I envision it, a mere Christendom would provide more real freedoms for the unbeliever than the current unbelieving society grants to believers. Measured by the Golden

Rule, when we evaluate our respective proposals, they have far less to worry about than I do.

But for some, it all comes down to sex. They want to keep the government "out of our bedrooms." What are they talking about? I have to live in their society, remember. And I built my house, which means I built my own bedroom. The government told me how far apart the studs had to be in my bedroom wall, they dictated how thick the sheetrock had to be, they mandated how far apart the sheetrock screws had to be, they had policies on the configuration of those sheetrock screws, they have laws on the size of the windows and what kind of glass I can have in them, and there are stern legal warnings on the mattress tags. What do you mean, you want to keep the government out of our bedrooms? The president is probably contemplating, right this minute, the establishment of a bedroom czar. And when he does, the usual suspects will be out there on the Sunday morning talk shows *defending* it. This is because secularists don't know what real freedom is. Their worldview doesn't have a slot for it.

# 10

# THE WEST IS DEAD.
# LONG LIVE THE WEST.

When theological folks dichotomize, they often do it without regard to the reality of *time*. And this causes no end of trouble.

Given their assumptions about the political dualities of life, the anabaptist impulse to reject infant baptism is a shrewd one, because all these things are connected together. And infant baptism is a statement, among other things, about *time*. The tangles we get into over visible Church/invisible Church, City of God/City of Man, Kingdom of God/kingdom of the devil, and Heaven/earth all occur because we try to conceive of them all as static realities and not as categories that exist in various forms of tension or battle over the course of history. Time matters; history matters. An infant you baptize is not the same person who goes to heaven, and yet is very much the same person. There is continuity and discontinuity, and much of it is revealed over time.

Some of us were baptized as infants, and some of us were not. But Western civilization certainly *was* baptized in infancy, and, as some might say, this accounts for many of the troubles we have had. I grant it, I acknowledge it. But the messiness of growing up to maturity is a messiness that (I would argue) God wants us to embrace.

The impulse to theological perfectionism is a deep one in every theological tradition because imperfect creatures such as ourselves like to believe that God's perfections are more like a proof out of Euclid than anything else. But God is perfect . . . not a perfectionist.

Perfectionists want static categories; they want things to be defined and to stay put. They want the kingdom of God to stay here, right where we put it, and they want the kingdom of man to stay right there, on the unbelieving shelf. And then Constantine converts. Darn.

## THE RISK OF SUCCEEDING

Maybe we can say he didn't really convert, and keep all our categories. Or maybe not. Once we have a king who professes Christ, we immediately have new and interesting dualities. He may have meant it and he might not have meant it. He could be a true Christian or a false one. More time goes by (what a pesky thing *time* is for theologians!), and then we have to consider another option. Maybe the magistrate is a true Christian, but an immature one. Maybe the Christian civilization he represents, baptized in infancy, is just going through the terrible twos, and now adolescence, and what next?

In that great gallery of the faith's heroes, Hebrews 11, we see the same kind of person, over and over again, but with different earthly outcomes. Since the city we are seeking, whose maker and builder is God, is not an earthly city, we are given a wide range of possibilities here. Those possibilities include both winning and losing.

There is a certain kind of servant—a worthless one, to use the words of his master—who wants to stay close to the shore, play it safe, take no great risks, and bury his talent in a napkin. This approach is taken by the cowardly who think their master is a "hard master."

In the parable of the talents, the risk-takers came back with more than they started with, but that doesn't *always* happen. The fellow who was given five talents made five more, and the man given two made two more (Mt. 25:14ff). But sometimes in our experience the man with five talents comes back with only three, and a little bit wiser. Nevertheless, the Lord praised the servants who were willing to lose.

R.L. Dabney refers somewhere to a pathetic kind of conservatism that has no intention of being guilty of the folly of martyrdom. But there is also a kind of conservatism that has no intention of running the risk of success. The same kind of timidity underlies both. But biblical faith always swings for the fence.

> And what shall I more say? for the time would fail me
> to tell of Gedeon, and of Barak, and of Samson, and of

Jephthae; of David also, and Samuel, and of the prophets: Who through faith subdued kingdoms, wrought
righteousness, obtained promises, stopped the mouths
of lions, Quenched the violence of fire, escaped the edge
of the sword, out of weakness were made strong, waxed
valiant in fight, turned to flight the armies of the aliens.
Women received their dead raised to life again: and others were tortured, not accepting deliverance; that they
might obtain a better resurrection: And others had tri-
al of cruel mockings and scourgings, yea, moreover of
bonds and imprisonment: They were stoned, they were
sawn asunder, were tempted, were slain with the sword:
they wandered about in sheepskins and goatskins; being
destitute, afflicted, tormented; (Of whom the world was
not worthy:) they wandered in deserts, and in moun-
tains, and in dens and caves of the earth. And these all,
having obtained a good report through faith, received
not the promise. (Heb. 11:32–39)

Some conquered kingdoms, and some were sawn in two.
Some stopped the mouths of lions, and some didn't. Some
turned armies to flight, and some were marched off to camps
by armies. Some quenched the violence of fire, and some were
stoned. Some turned five talents into five hundred, while others had their one remaining talent emptied from their pocket
before they were tied to the stake. But all of them overcame
by faith.

The cowardice that is afraid of success is not biblical faith,
and it will be that same lack of faith that, when it comes to
the point, refuses to pay the price that a martyr would pay.

Faith is willing for earthly success *or* failure, whatever the Lord has ordained for us. Cowardice is ultimately willing for neither, because cowardice won't take the risk of failure that is necessary in order for real success to occur. Faint heart . . . fair lady, and it became a proverb because it is *true*.

Health-and-wealthers want only the possibility of success. Doom-and-gloomers want only the possibility of ongoing failure. But biblical faith knows what it wants, and what it *ultimately* wants is not in this world anyway. Because the final reward is found in the resurrection, in the city to come, and not here, *we are set free to attempt great things here.* To different kinds of cowardice this looks positively reckless, but reckless in different ways. Some are afraid that our psalm singing will wake up the lions, while others are afraid that the psalm singing will stop the mouths of those same lions.

In the words of one insightful business executive, we must remember that "nothing is ever accomplished by a reasonable man." Socrates famously said that he was the wisest man among the Greeks because he knew of his ignorance. Let us riff off this Socratic insight if we may, if riff is a term recognized by the philosophers. We are all smaller than tiny. We all have a tiny role to play, and the fact that we are tiny makes our duties tiny—without making them unimportant. How God did that, I don't know, but He did.

The gift of God enables us to take our graces and duties seriously without taking *ourselves* seriously. Those suffering along without this gift either neglect their graces and duties, or pursue their duties raw precisely because they take

themselves very seriously indeed. Here is the Socratic riff.
They are unimportant because they do not understand themselves to be unimportant. Those who understand how small
we are, and how unimportant we all are—ah, those are the
important ones. Keep an eye on them.

I once had the privilege of debating David Niose, president of the American Humanist Association. The debate was
sponsored by the fine folks in the Federalist Society at Liberty University Law School, and we were debating whether
Christianity or humanism provided the better path for culture, law, politics, and so forth. I was advocating, naturally,
mere Christendom.

Mr. Niose, who struck me as a very nice man, said in the
course of the debate that the Bible was a tired and ancient
book, with a bunch of irrelevant laws, citing as one example
the Old Testament prohibition of eating shellfish. In my reply, I pointed to the stark alternative this presented—a faith
in which the adherents were at one time prohibited from
eating shellfish, and on the other hand a faith in which the
adherents used to *be* shellfish.

Now this got a laugh, and his response illustrated the point
I was making above. My passing joke elicited from him his
most urgent and pressing point, to wit, the intellectual *sanctity*
of the theory of evolution. I've said enough about that theory
already, so I will pass by it here, noting only in that passing
my agreement with Malcolm Muggeridge that, in retrospect,
evolution will be known as one of the great jokes of history.
My point here has to do with the issue of self-importance.

The secular state is an over-inflated balloon, and when the right moment comes, the tiniest joke, as told by someone like Martin Luther, with the teeniest little sharp point, should do the trick.

On paper, you would think that an evolutionist would understand that the entire human race is just as meaningless as the froth in a storm on one of Jupiter's molten seas. Both phenomena put on a show for nonexistent spectators, and then the lights go out. You would think that someone who *thought* that would have a deep sense of how trivial everything is, up to and including the prospect of every last Supreme Court justice being one day a graduate of Liberty University Law School. But no . . .

Now I don't mean to indicate that the Christian faith is devoid of self-important fussers. Alack and alas! But at least our fussers have absolutely no excuse. They have memorized the Heidelberg Catechism in the original Greek, and so they should know.

Such perspective is the grace of God, and if there is no God, goodbye to any such perspective. But because the triune God is infinite, and the Second Person of that Trinity became one of us, insignificance and cosmic importance now indwell one another, world without end. Amen.

## OUR OWN LONG MARCH

In chapter three of *To Change the World*, James Hunter offers his criticism of popular evangelical cultural engagement. One of his points, the fact that evangelicals do not have a robust enough understanding of the role of the Church in all this, is well taken, and needs to be made again and again. But there is another sense in which I don't believe that Hunter can see what evangelicals are actually doing.

He represents the popular evangelical view of cultural change as being the idea that if you reach enough individuals with evangelism, and then follow-up discipleship in "Christian worldview thinking," those individuals in the aggregate will then percolate through society, naturally transforming it. His critique of this is that evangelicals are thus *"ignoring the institutional nature of culture and disregarding the way culture is embedded in structures of power."*[142]

Now I am, so to speak, a reformational and evangelical Gramscian. I believe that we should have our own "long march through the institutions." I agree with Hunter completely that leaving institutions and elites out of a proposed reformational solution is futile and wrongheaded.

I also agree with Hunter that cultural change is not the result of a simple equation between the number of individuals who think or believe a certain way and their culture then reflecting those same values. Democracy cheats. Hunter points out the disproportionate influence that homosexuals have had on our culture,[143] which most certainly was not the result of them getting past a magical tipping point in the demographics. They succeeded, to use an old phrase of Gary North's, by "capturing the gowns"—the mainline seminaries, the courts,

---

142  Hunter, 27. Emphasis his.
143  Ibid., 20.

the university. Theirs has been an institutional victory, and the gowns they captured were also *fabulous*.

Hunter also points to the stubborn facts behind Jewish cultural influence. Less than five percent of the population is Jewish, and their cultural contributions are "both brilliant and unrivaled."[144] This, in the face of a significant prejudice against them. And it is a tenacious kind of prejudice, the kind that uses your very successes as evidence that "you must be cheating whenever you win." But the apostle Paul's strategy, one that he assigned to *us*, was to provoke the Jews to cultural envy, and to be provoked to envy by *them*, instead, is about the most un-Pauline thing we could think up to do. The achievements of Jews have been far more than political, and have included "science, literature, art, music, letters, film, and architecture."[145] The apostle Paul argues that the salvation of the world depends on Christians figuring out the riposte to this.

Now in order to have disproportionate influence like this, a group has to be using levers or, at the very least, perhaps their heads.

In all this, Hunter is making some important points. But here is where he is missing something important, where I think he gets off on the wrong foot. There are many ways to approach this, so I will use just a couple of examples.

I have been a foot soldier in the culture wars for over forty years now. In that time, I have seen enough exasperating examples from within the evangelical ranks to give Hunter's

144  Ibid.
145  Ibid.

point more than a footnote or two. But one thing that Hunter gets entirely wrong is this central point of his about building institutions. For virtually that entire time, I have been in the good company of many thousands of Christians who have been planting *institutions*—schools, for one instance. Sometimes I think it is all we do. Private Christian education is a network of institutions, many hundreds of them, and virtually all of them under fifty years old. Within that is the classical Christian movement. There is now an Association of Classical Christian Schools with hundreds of member schools; in early 1980, there weren't any. Then in the realm of higher education, there is New St. Andrews, and Patrick Henry College, and you get the point. Something important to evangelicals is driving all this, and for some reason it is invisible to Hunter.

Even where Hunter's point is most strong (on the question of Church proper, and worship), some very heartening things have been happening—many churches have also been planted within the last generation with the self-conscious understanding that it is worship that drives the world. Man is *homo adorans*—not *homo sapiens* in the first instance.

Here is my second example. Even at the broad parachurch level, where Hunter's point seems to be most cogent, groups like *Focus on the Family* are fighting against homosexual marriage, for example, and in favor of the biblical definition of marriage. Now when they are doing this, they have risen in defense of an *institution*. Marriage is not an assigned arrangement of roommates with sexual privileges. It is one of the fundamental *institutions*.

Our secularists are currently attempting something that Nero never dreamed of. Now this fight is a defensive one, granted, but it remains an institutional one. The guys in the Alamo might well *lose* the fight they are in, but it would be misguided to tap one of them on the shoulder and tell him that they weren't paying enough attention to the importance of defending small mission buildings in San Antonio.

In short, the famous and vaunted individualism of the evangelical is being overstated here. Human beings are inescapably institution-builders, and evangelicals are above average in this respect. They have the spiritual energy to start institutions up. Liberals know how to capture and crash planes, but believers do know how to build them. We do, however, need to get better at defending what we have built, I grant that.

Now a concluding point. An airplane in the construction hanger at Boeing *does not fly nearly as well* as an airplane in the sky, captured by the secularist jihadis, who are going to crash it into the skyscraper of civilization to the defiant cry of "Orgasm Akbar!" Sometimes my illustrations just take on a life of their own. Nothing I can do about it.

## TOP DOWN REFORMS

Hunter writes, "But my question is not so much about the residual effects of a once robust and pervasive Christianity that continues to define the contours and character of American society but about the capacity of present-day Christianity to reproduce itself in ways that influence the larger world for good."[146]

146  Ibid., 79.

The question concerns where contemporary Christians are situated in our culture and what sort of limit that situation places on their capacity (important word) to exert real cultural influence.

In an earlier chapter, Hunter had indicated his view that cultures are changed from the top *down*, and from central institutions *out*. While this is clearly not the whole story (as Hunter also acknowledges), it remains an important part of the discussion. And near the end of this chapter, where Hunter shows how far away from the top evangelicals are, and how far out on the margins they are, he says that this is why nothing profound is going to change anytime soon.

"Against the prevailing view, the main reason why Christian believers today (from various communities) have not had the influence in the culture to which they have aspired is not that they don't believe enough or try hard enough or care enough to think Christianly enough or have the right worldview, but rather *because they have been absent from the arenas in which the greatest influence in the culture is exerted.*"[147]

In response to all this, I would want to make two basic points. The first has to do with his use of the word "capacity" in the first citation; the second with his use of the phrase "they have been absent" in the second. A lot rides on both of them—not only on the accuracy of the statements, but on the reasons that might be given for the accuracy.

First, capacity is a very different thing in a uniform situation and in a fluctuating situation. Just as the evolutionary

147  Ibid., 89, emphasis his.

framework doesn't have intellectual room for catastrophes like a global flood, so also the gradual decline into cultural apostasy doesn't have room for convulsive reformations or revivals. The unbelieving mind loves to think this way. Not only is the road to Hell paved with good intentions, but the whole thing is on a slight slope downward, two degrees at the most, and no runaway truck ramps are needed—"since the fathers fell asleep, all things continue as they were from the beginning of the creation" (2 Pet. 3:4). Because the unbelieving mind is all about control, uniformitarianism is the most helpful way for the unbelieving mind to maintain the illusion of that control for itself. This pervasive assumption in the unbelieving world easily affects Christian scholars like Hunter who assume that "nothing is going to change at this rate," which is quite true. But why do they assume that "this rate" is a constant, like the speed of light?

The biblical story shows us this pattern again and again. This is God training us to think about history. God delivers His people, God's people rejoice, God's people forget Him and worship idols, God chastises them by bringing them into affliction, the people cry out to God, and God delivers His people. Rinse and repeat.

Now there is an important qualification that has to be made about this pattern. There is a linear aspect to history, and there is a cyclic aspect to it. The linear aspect is fundamental, and the cycles are subordinate to that line. The line, overall, is going up, which means that each repeated cycle represents a new advance—we are better off at the end of the tenth cycle than we were at the end of the third one. To put it in tangible terms,

we were far better off at the conclusion of Whitefield's awak-
enings than we were at the end of King Josiah's reformation.
Postmillennial thinking does not require us to believe that the
kingdom improves every day in every way, or that the whole
thing takes off like the space shuttle. It is more like five steps
forward, three steps back, seven steps forward, six back, three
steps forward, one step forward, and then two steps back.

What this means is that Christianity has latent "capacities"
that have burst forth many times in Church history, but which
are not bursting forth most of the time in Church history.
When it happens, historians fall into the common scholarly
sin of thinking that description is explanation, and the fact
that they can show the antecedents to the Reformation now
does not mean that they would have been able to predict the
Reformation had they been given seats on the fifty-yard-line
in 1516. Instead, the Spirit came upon Luther, and all of sud-
den a number of impossible things began to happen. God
has *always* done it this way, and when He does it the next
time, we will be as surprised as we always are. The *capacity* of
the Christian faith to introduce major transformations with
little advance warning resembles the capacity of volcanoes in
Iceland to do the same thing.

My second point concerns the curious use of the phrase
"they have been absent." On the facts of the case, Hunter
is quite right. Christians have been absent from the citadels
of power. Why? Because the secularists are vigilant to guard
their gates and police their corridors. If I have "been absent"
from work, the *reasons* for this should be noted. It matters

whether I am at home in bed pretending to be sick so that I can watch the big game or if I am in a strange house helping my captors make the ransom video.

In a sense, this observation is true, but only in a tautological way—it is as though one GI says to another one on the beaches of Normandy, "You know, the only reason we are stuck behind this sand dune like this is because we haven't captured Berlin yet." Well, yeah.

America has been the scene of raucous culture wars from the beginning. Yale was founded because Harvard had gone bad, and Princeton was a refuge for evangelicals after Yale had gone bad. In these culture wars, both sides know about the war, and both sides are fighting it. The issue is not trying to convince Christians to simply gravitate to certain influential spots. Those spots are *defended*, and defended by a canny and fierce enemy.

So it's not as though Christians could just stroll into the important cultural centers or walk in unimpeded provided they were willing to do the work. Dr. Robert George once spoke for New St. Andrews' commencement, and at a dinner we had for him, a colleague asked how he managed, um, to get by at Princeton, being as outspokenly conservative as he was. He replied that it was with both guns blazing—and that he advises young academics to do the same thing. If you keep your head down, they will find you anyway, and then when "the hit" comes, all you have done is provide your adversaries with plausible deniability. *Lots* of people don't get tenure, ya know?

Christians know all about the influential centers that Hunter talks about—and have known about them for a long time. I have been privileged to know a number of faithful Christians who have gotten graduate degrees from prestigious universities, and it really was a dicey proposition for them. Others keep their heads down and manage to survive—but the price tag is one of personal compromise. When they get to a position of influence, they can't use it, because they discover that they misplaced their soul somewhere along the way. Or they fly the flag nobly, and are taken out. A mere handful survive without compromise because the machine gun fire is withering. Anybody who thinks that the secularists don't guard their prize institutions ferociously is being naive. But I understand what they are doing—they *have* to guard them because a large number of Christians have them under siege.

Remember what happened to that poor editor sentry at the Smithsonian journal who let some Intelligent Design guy publish a peer-reviewed paper? It was thunder, lightning, and blue ruin.

## ESCHATOLOGY READS THE WHOLE BOOK

The walls of the Church are permeable, and this is by God's design. This means that when the Church is being the Church, there is no way to keep the influence of this from seeping into the world. On the flip side, when the Church has lost her vision or her focus, or they have kept both but only in the confessional documents, this means that the influence of the world will seep into the Church.

Some church bodies seek to address this problem by removing the permeability of the walls. The church assumes a bunker mentality, which is just another way of saying that it has become a sect. The other response is to abandon all efforts at keeping the church functioning self-consciously as the Church, and instead of seeping in, the world floods in.

Liberal churches are those that welcome the world in. "Conservative" churches tend to build thick walls to keep the world out of the Church and, just as importantly, to keep the Church out of the world.

Then there are the clueless—ever among us!—who in the name of influencing the world do very little else than follow the world around like an adoring fanboy. You find them outside the theater where the latest Tarantino is playing, smoking cigarettes on the sidewalk, and if you ask them what they are doing, it will involve an appeal to Kuyperianism somehow.

The Church must focus on being the Church. Our first order of business is reformation in the Church. But we are not fleeing the center of society when we do this because worship of the true God is the true center of every society. God cannot be worshiped rightly in any culture without that worship challenging and dislocating all idolatries. To focus on the right worship of God is to declare war, it is to throw down the gauntlet.

This is because when we worship God rightly, we have ascended into the heavenly places in order to glorify the name of Jesus Christ. He is glorified in Heaven, and then we ask, in humble faith, for God to glorify His name on earth as it has just been glorified in heaven. This is something that God is pleased to do, and this is why we ask for His kingdom to *come*, not for His kingdom to *go*.

We have different styles of approach to this problem. As all the different forms of Christian engagement with the world have gathered on our front lawn, we see the conservatives on the right side, the progressives on the left side, and the anabaptists off in the bushes. Hunter helpfully discusses the respective forms of engagement advocated by each. As Hunter breaks it down, they are "defensive against" from the conservatives, "relevance to" from the libs, and "purity from" with the anabaptists.

Hunter is not talking about a conceptual construct (like Niebuhr's), but rather he is speaking to the historically specific circumstances here in North America. And I think he gets it basically right. Missing from the list is the one I would like to see, which is "evangelization and discipleship of the nations therein," but you can't have everything. Not enough North Americans have signed up for that one yet, although in just a minute we will address why they really ought.

With regard to these responses, Hunter says, "In sum, all three paradigms capture something important to the experience, life, identity, and witness of the church."[148] This is quite correct, but we still have to move back a step. Each one of these engagement paradigms is driven by certain assumptions about the nature of history, and so we still need to know what the respective points of the defense, relevance,

148  Hunter, 223.

and purity are. *By what standard? To what end?* The Church and the unbelieving culture are not two static realities that have to be balanced somehow, but are rather characters in a story. The Church and culture are not two pieces of furniture that have to be permanently arranged in accordance with the laws of *feng shui*. Rather, the relationship between them has to be balanced through a narrative line, straight through to the conclusion. And it matters greatly what that conclusion is. What happens in the final chapters?

What good is it if soldiers are defending the fort if they don't know what the war is over? What good is it to be relevant to the world if you don't know what end that relevance is supposed to achieve? And why separate from the world if you don't know why that separation is a good thing? In short, all these questions are teleological, and you can't discuss teleology in history with Christians without talking about eschatology.

I really do believe that we in the Church should defend against the world's encroachments, because we are involved in a spiritual war. In this war, I believe also that we are to show the relevance of living in the way we do so that more and more non-Christians will hear the gospel, lay down their arms, and surrender to Jesus Christ. In order to do this in a way that is not compromised, it is necessary to stay separate from the standards of the world. We are commanded not to love the world or the baubles found in the world. All three of Hunter's forms of engagement are true, but if they are not related to the task of discipling the nations because Jesus is now Lord of all the nations, then *each* of the three will get radically out of kilter.

The conservatives will wind up defending their hidebound ways, just because we always did this; the progressives will wind up throwing all their virgins into the volcano of the state, just like they always do; the anabaptists will wind up confounding prophetic courage and snarky ingratitude. Defending, relating, and separating are all connected to transitive verbs, and, as we've repeatedly noted, no virtue or vice can be found in a transitive verb. Everything hinges on what you are defending and why. Everything depends on what you are relevant to and why. Everything revolves around what you are separating from and why.

The *why* here needs to be the conversion of the world. All the families of the earth were promised to Abraham, and all our strategies should be tied in with advancing our ability to proclaim that glorious and *conquering* reality to them. The root of Jesse has been planted, and all the nations of the Gentiles will in fact trust in Him. Everything we do, all day long, should dovetail with that understanding. As we read the novel that God is writing, how the denouement is supposed to come down is not a trifle. It should be the key to understanding the structure of the whole book.

## APPLICATION AND THE WORLD OUTSIDE THE CHURCH

In a chapter titled "The Bragging Calvinist," Jason Stellman lays down some good basic principles. He sticks close to the text of Scripture, and shows how bragging in your own autonomous glory apart from the Lord is excluded, and how the new covenant opens up new freedoms in which we may voluntarily submit ourselves to situations that God did not require of us, and boast righteously in that. And ultimately, of course, let him who boasts do so in the Lord. But the devil is in the details, and differences arise when we come to application.

When a congregation asks for applicatory preaching, they are asking to be taught how to *live*. Jason Stellman objects to this: "This request is often tantamount to a desire for law instead of gospel, a hunger to be told what we can do for God rather than resting in what He has done for us . . . But the gospel is never an assumption from within but always an announcement from without, which is why we need to be trained to long for gospel rather than law."[149]

Now I actually agree with this, as far as it goes, but I think this is not being cynical enough about the propensity of human beings to turn *anything* whatever into law. We can even do this with the words of grace, and the higher the octane of the grace, the greater the wrong kind of pride when the twisting comes. The thing that saves is *actual grace*, not grace formally noted and applauded. Our trust in Christ is found in the heart of the prayer, and not in whether or not the footnotes of the prayer are doctrinally proper and according to Turabian. The Pharisee who went down to the Temple to pray gave credit where credit was due. He actually prayed a *soli Deo gloria* prayer, did he not? "I thank thee, *God*, that I am not like other men . . . ."

149  Stellman, 160.

Whenever you preach practical application—like the apostle Paul consistently does at the conclusion of his letters—it is quite possible and, depending on the people, highly likely that they will turn this into a new law and then impale themselves on it. Yes, people do that, and they do it when the Holy Spirit is not active in sparing them from that particular folly. But you can't get away from this tendency by knocking off the applicatory preaching. In order to knock it off, you have to urge one another to knock off the application so that we are not distracted into works righteousness, and whenever you urge people to do something like that, a bunch of them *will apply what you say.* And we all know how dangerous application is.

For a legal heart, everything is law. For a gracious heart, everything is grace. When the Spirit is moving among a people, you do not stumble them by telling them how to love their wives, bring up their children, work hard at their jobs, and so on. No reason to snip out the last three chapters of Ephesians. And if the Spirit is not moving among a people, you cannot keep them safe in "grace" by insisting upon no ethical obligations whatever. What could go wrong with that, right?

The proclamation of grace without an actual movement of the Spirit's grace is nothing but tiny works, cerebral works, the work of sitting on your butt listening to sermons about it. *That's a work* . . . for the wrong kind of heart. The experience of grace is the death and resurrection of Jesus Christ actually saving people. Of course, we tell them about it—how will they hear without a preacher—but salvation is not found in the telling, the hearing, the willing or the running. Salvation is found in the saving; salvation is as salvation does, and salvation does what God tells it to. And when salvation comes, one of the remarkable things is that the Reformed get reformed, and evangelicals get born again.

Suppose we listen to the good news proclaimed about a salvation accomplished outside Jerusalem two thousand years ago, and it is all outside of me and all my straining efforts. Suppose we listen to it, hear, and heed. And suppose further that my life still has sixty years left in it—now what? Practical teaching from the Scriptures is teaching that is grounded in the text of Scripture, and is therefore protected from becoming a false gospel to the extent that the last three chapters of Ephesians—do this and not that—are grounded in the first three chapters. The most important word in that book is *therefore*, right at the beginning of chapter 4. *Therefore*, do these things. People who do them or preach doing them, but who don't *therefore* do them, *are disobeying the gospel*. And those who luxuriate in the redemptive historical sweep of the first three chapters, but don't let the sermon series get into labor relations, Christian marriage, Christian education, church government, and so forth, are also *disobeying the gospel*. Whenever you see a *therefore*, what's it there for?

## THE GOSPEL WITH THE CLUTCH IN

When we look at what is happening to the culture around us, and we recognize that so much of the destruction is avoidable, and we consider also the fact that the people implementing these suicidal policies are not idiots—and indeed exhibit an intelligence of the highest order in other areas—the conclusion appears inescapable. Our problems are spiritual. They are the sort of moral problems that have always afflicted—pardon the use of an anachronism—sinners.

Sinners always want salvation. The damned don't want salvation—that is what it means to be damned. But sinners aren't there yet, and so they are always casting about in search of a savior. Of course it has to be a flattering savior, one who will be whispering soothing words on the way to the bad place. This is because sinners want to be damned, sort of, eventually. At least they prefer approaching damnation to the only alternative, which is a real Savior, that is to say, Jesus. And their preference stays this way unless a real Savior intervenes.

This is not just true on the individual level—although it certainly is true there. We are social beings, which means that while we get into to Heaven or Hell by ones, we travel there in groups and clusters. Civilizations are what they are because we, within those civilizations, think the same way about things. Among these things we should include the topics of sin and salvation.

Put this another way. There is no way to preach the gospel clearly to an American without also preaching what *America* needs. And if you are not preaching what America needs, what you are declaring ain't gonna save nobody in particular. Of course, considering the way many preachers declare the gospel these days, that may be (secretly) the point.

There are any number of ways to take what I am about to say in the wrong way, so I would like to begin with a request that nobody do that. But this will not happen because what I am about to say is inherently confusing. It is because it is self-evidently and manifestly true, and true in a way that brings shame. When men are ashamed by truth, the first and most obvious thing to do is "misunderstand" that which convicted them, and to misconstrue it.

That said . . . we are having Reformed convulsions within the Church about redemptive-historical preaching falsely set over against "application" because we are ashamed of Jesus. Application in one's personal life might lead people to think that such applications might be possible even if a parishioner were a governor or a congressman. And who knows where *that* might lead?

Redemptive-historical preaching, as commended by many today, is like teaching lifeguards to get swimmers off the bottom of the pool, but to be sure to behave thereafter as though getting them dry and breathing the air presents a constant temptation to moralism. It requires preachers to act as though the first three chapters of Ephesians had been written by the apostle Paul and the last three chapters contributed by Dale Carnegie.

We are warned in Scripture against that which we are in danger of committing. When John tells his dear children to keep themselves from idols, he tells them this because they might not keep themselves from doing that. We are told to love our wives because there will be temptations to love ourselves instead. And, coming back to the point just made, we are cautioned against the sin of being ashamed of Jesus and His words. What are those words? They are the words

He gave us to teach to all the nations after we had baptized them. Why are we cautioned this way? Because there will be a temptation for Christians to be ashamed of Jesus, that's why.

What does the Lord say?

> And he straitly charged them, and commanded them to tell no man that thing; Saying, The Son of man must suffer many things, and be rejected of the elders and chief priests and scribes, and be slain, and be raised the third day. And he said to them all, If any man will come after me, let him deny himself, and take up his cross daily, and follow me. For whosoever will save his life shall lose it: but whosoever will lose his life for my sake, the same shall save it. For what is a man advantaged, if he gain the whole world, and lose himself, or be cast away? For whosoever shall be ashamed of me and of my words, of him shall the Son of man be ashamed, when he shall come in his own glory, and in his Father's, and of the holy angels. (Luke 9:21–26)

Note first that Jesus said that He was going to be rejected by all the most important graduates of all the most important seminaries. He was going to be rejected by the elders and the chief priests and the scholars. Anybody who follows Him needs to be prepared for the same treatment—needs to take up his cross. He who tries to juggle keeping his own life with keeping Jesus will lose both. Now what does denying one-self entail? Could this possibly include academic reputation? Denominational standing? The right connections at the right publishing houses? To ask the question is to answer it.

And Jesus equates this kind of fearful heart with being ashamed of Him. To say that the words of Jesus apply to absolutely everything—for He is, remember, Lord of all—is a recipe for trouble.

I am not addressing these words to those diehards in that redemptive-historical world who really believe what they have been taught. I am actually talking to those who are situated in such contexts, but who know that what I am saying is *true*. They know, further, that the only reason they are keeping quiet is that they would be ashamed to be identified with a position that has had so much opprobrium heaped on it. And believe me, the lordship of Jesus over everything will *always* have opprobrium heaped on it. Who wants to be a nutter? Keep it respectable, champ. Keep your head down. Read those books, certainly. Enjoy them in your study, friend. No harm in that, but don't go to extremes. Keep your head down.

The only difficulty is that it is hard to preach with any kind of authority when you've got your head down. It doesn't work that way.

Change the metaphor. Redemptive-historical preaching without application to every aspect of life, preaching without declaring all things subject to the authority of Jesus, is revving the engine with the clutch in. One can be quite a powerful presence in the pulpit. *Vroom, vroom.*

## JUDICIAL BLINDNESS

When societies fall apart, they do not do so in an orderly manner. When God strikes a people with a judicial stupor,

the result is not a feast of reason and flow of soul. "For the
Lord hath poured out upon you the spirit of deep sleep, and
hath closed your eyes: the prophets and your rulers, the seers
hath he covered" (Is. 29:10).

But when God does this thing, the people under the judgment would have it so. They murmur *amen* as they roll over
for some more shuteye. "Which say to the seers, See not; and
to the prophets, Prophesy not unto us right things, speak unto
us smooth things, prophesy deceits" (Is. 30:10).

And when this happens, the pomomush gets mushier, and
the conservative responses get increasingly bewildered and
ineffective. The conservative gets out his sharp knife of dialectical analysis in order to carve up a bowl of soup.

Once the intellectual dishonesty has gotten to this stage
(as it certainly has in our society), our response must be to
turn to the scattered flocks that have seen their shepherds go
mad, *and preach the gospel to them.* And as we undertake this
crucial task, we should not make common cause with any of
the raving shepherds.

The Jews can get all the signs they could want, and the
Greeks might get all the wisdom that a fifty-pound book
of philosophy could hold, but at the end they still wouldn't
know God. The modernists might get all the technological
geewhizzery they can invent, and still not know God. They
did not find the Lord in outer space, and they did not find
Him in the microchip. The postmodernists might get all the
sexual license that every one of their arguments leads to . . .

and they would not know God. They did not find Him in any their pomosexualities.

We do not look to the modernists for anything but stainless steel despair. Bigger, faster, shinier! And we do not look to the pomos for anything but bootless confusions. When you finally get that quorum of clowns, *you are going to have a circus*. What did you expect?

Societies need to know God just as individuals do. If a society does not know the true God, the only God, then they will commune with idols. When they commune with idols, nothing good comes from it. You cannot, Christian, dispense with the Savior and keep the salvation. When Jesus Christ is declared to them, *in their office of nationhood*, the biblical process of biblical transformation gets underway. *If not, then not.* Jesus said to preach to every creature. Jesus said to baptize the nations. Jesus said to disciple the nations. Whatever do you suppose He meant by it?

The means that He ordained for the conversion of this sorry excuse for a world was the folly of preaching. We will not bring this about because we have reached into our arsenal and pulled out our armies and navies, our parliaments, our laws, and our ivy-covered halls of learning. The next Christendom will come to be when Christian preachers speak it into existence through the folly of preaching. See? I must be clean out of my mind.

## AMERICA'S UNKNOWN GOD

A city can be teeming with idols, as Athens was, and yet retain something in its history that provides a foothold for preaching the truth. This is what the apostle Paul did when he preached that their unknown god was in fact the true God (Acts 17:23). But the altar he took his preaching cue from was not an altar set up by Abraham or Moses. The altar was set up in obedience to direction by Epimenides, the Cretan prophet who had been summoned to help the Athenians deal with a great plague. The plague was successfully stopped when the Athenians sacrificed to this god. In one place Paul himself calls Epimenides a prophet (Tit. 1:12) and identifies the god worshiped by the Athenians in ignorance as the true God.

One of the reasons why Protestant missionaries were so successful in Korea is that the Koreans had a "most high" God named *Hananim* who was virtually unknown to the Koreans, and the missionaries preached Jesus as the Son of Hananim. This is different than trying the same tactic with Muslims and their Allah, because (as a Christian heresy) Islam has defined Allah as the one who can have no Son. In Muslim lands, Allah is an idol. Hananim was an unknown God.

While this distinction must be made, at the same time we must not be superstitious about words. The Coptic Christians use the word Allah for God the Father—and it was their word for Him before there were any Muslims. And Paul, in that famous exchange with the Athenians, says that "we are all his offspring," quoting from a hymn to *Zeus* (Acts 17:28). This was lawful because there was a difference between the

Homeric Zeus with his sexual hijinks and the Zeus of the philosophers. The Zeus of the philosophers was Hananim— think for a minute about the similarities between *Deus*, *Theos*, and *Zeus*.

So this brings us to the God of American civil religion. Is he an idol or not? I used to believe so, but I have changed my mind about this. I believe it would be far better for us to say that he is an unknown god and to preach the gospel to Americans, telling them that this God has made Himself known in the revelation of Jesus Christ.

This is not to say that there is no *attempted* idolatry involved. There is, and the secularists are insistent that we keep it that way. There is a difference between an unknown god (who may then be declared and revealed by faithful preachers) and placeholder higher being force, a blank screen where all the citizens may project their own personal understanding of the deity (with the tacit understanding that all other religions will be allowed to project their understanding of the deity onto that same screen). This latter approach really is idolatrous, and this placeholder deity spot is subordinate to the true god of the system, which is of course the *state*. At the same time, as an attempted strategy, this approach really is *very recent*.

Paul preached the God that Epimenides had had the Athenians sacrifice to centuries before. If he did that, why cannot Christian preachers declare that the God on our money, the one in whom we trust, gave us His Son so that we might *genuinely* trust in Him? Why can we not preach that the phrase "under God" was added to the Pledge of Allegiance in the 1950s in response to pressure by *evangelicals*, who were talking about the true God? The only way for a nation to be under God is by means of mediator—who is Christ. It is the job of Christian preachers to declare that "what you did not know" is "now made manifest." This is not the task of legislators, incidentally; it is the job of *preachers*.

When we do this, we are not surrendering the exclusive claims that Christ places upon the title of *Lord*. This proclamation fills up the space that idolaters wanted to create for any "god as you conceive him/her/it to be." We are preaching Christ, the only way to salvation. We want Jesus to be recognized as Lord, and we want Him to be recognized as Lord by Americans. In this task, we are not starting from scratch. We are drilling deep into the collective memory of Americans.

There was a time when this God, unknown to this current generation, was known to our fathers. How do we get back there? We get there through Jesus. Jesus is the only way to the Father. He is also the only way to anything good and true. Jesus is the only way back.

.

www.ingramcontent.com/pod-product-compliance
Lightning Source LLC
Chambersburg PA
CBHW062049270326
41931CB00013B/3000